Maff Potts has spent 30 years working in the social justice sector. This included turning the Millennium Dome into a homeless shelter; running the biggest homeless service in the UK; building a new generation of homeless centres in England for the British Government; and being CEO of a national charity and a housing association.

Maff left traditional forms of social change in 2015 when he started the social movement Camerados in his bedroom. As of January 2025 there are 260 Public Living Rooms in 6 countries worldwide, in libraries, hospitals, parks, community centres—wherever the community can find space and a sofa or two. Maff is also a jazz piano player, co-founder of a jazz club and has, for many years, run an after-school club for 8 - 11 year olds called "Funky Friday".

www.camerados.org

Victoria Herriman is an illustrator, designer, and arts activist who believes in the power of creativity and humour to bring people together. Her journey hasn't always been easy, but it's one shaped by resilience and a deep belief that art can inspire, connect, and make a difference. Whether working on community projects, creating space for random conversations, or simply sitting down to share a brew, Victoria's focus is always on people and finding the right hat for the occasion.

www.victoriaherriman.com

Any profits from this book
go directly to support the
work of the Camerados
movement

FRIENDS AND PURPOSE

Stories from sofas on streets
and some *confounding ideas*
for tough times

Maff Potts

Drawings by Victoria Herriman

GOMETRA

Published by Roc Sandford at the
Gometra Press in February 2025
Text © Maff Potts 2025
Drawings and Photos © Camerados
Design and Typesetting by Roc Sandford © Camerados
Set in Eric Gill's Golden Cockerel and
Ryoichi Tsunekawa's **BEBAS NEUE**.
Format Royal Octavo
Paperback printed on 50lb white paper
Cloth printed on 70lb cream paper
This edition dated 28/01/25
Printed and bound by IngramSpark
Cloth ISBN 978-1-906180-28-7
Paper ISBN 978-1-906180-29-4

This book is dedicated to —

Ruth,

Jenny Fox,

And all the camerados on the streets who shared their stories in this book.

TOWNS

IDEAS

HASTINGS

Ethel sat down and immediately made an impression. Small burgundy box hat and a black veil over her face like she was going to a mafia wedding. In her seventies maybe, small features, tiny body and a quizzical, uncertain feeling towards the whole sofa-on-a-street thing that quickly dissipated as soon as she joined me, got used to it, and pulled a blanket over her legs.

There was no small talk with Ethel. "My children want to control me," she said. "They think they know what's best for me. I wish people would stop. Just stop." Pause. "Stop bloody well telling me what to do." The Hastings wind howled around us a bit, she pulled the blanket further up her body and her eyes watered but I don't think it was tears, just the coldness all around her. "I mean I'm very thankful but I keep telling them that all I want to do is sing." "Really?" I said. "Yes, it is the only thing that makes me happy. I'm in a little choir. But they don't think I'm up to going each week. I'm fed up." She smiled when she talked about the choir. We discussed their repertoire and she gave me a little song, a rendition of Gershwin's "Our love is here to stay", which was quiet but passionately felt and whisked away by the wind leaving passers by with a smile breaking on their lips and a knowing glance or two in our direction. Her eyes were piercing, cold ice blue and actually felt angry even though she was not shouting at me. She just stared at me intensely. "I can do things, you know," she said, looking for my reaction. I nodded. "I have no doubt," I offered rather lamely. Then suddenly she got up and left, saying she'd come back later and give me another song, but sadly she never did. I wish I'd been a little more encouraging to her.

Alan is stocky with a khaki jacket from an army surplus store. Skin rough and red like he'd sand-papered it. He talked in short sharp phrases as if he was suppressing anger all the time, though in our time together he seemed very soft and kind. "Can I help you with that sofa?" "Anybody want a Steak Bake from Greggs?".

When he talked it felt like he wanted to project a macho persona but his nerves betrayed him. He confessed that he struggled with his confidence around people. He liked Wetherspoons cos he could sit with a coffee as long as he liked and nobody would bother him. That was the main thing Alan wanted, people to just "get it" and back off. He didn't want to have to explain how messed up his head was all the time, even though it was. He made it clear that his time in the military was not a happy time – I sensed it was traumatic, even – and yet he still wore his insignia proudly and showed me tattoos all over his arms dedicated to his regiment. I found that odd but interpreted it to be about a sense of belonging and identity. He loved the people, not the job maybe, which I took from how he behaved the moment someone else joined us. He chatted to others and was kind and responsive to their conversations. Yet when the subject turned back to him it got dark quickly, his demeanour changed and eventually he just slipped away, I suspect to Wetherspoons. I wanted to tell him that in Hastings, just up the road, there was a permanent public living room open every day and that it was also a place where, like 'Spoons,' nobody would get in his face just without the cheap alcohol from 8 in the morning. But I didn't tell him that because today he just needed company and maybe I felt that even offering this advice would be seen as "getting in his face". Company was enough.

Two Camerados from the local public living room arrived to show me a bit of solidarity. "I felt the icy wind and thought, I better go and give him some company out there," one said. I was profoundly touched by this because I knew both of them had some pretty tough back stories and I wouldn't blame them for not trusting people easily. Yet, despite meeting me just for one day earlier that week, they showed up to sit on the sofa with me, and I felt distinctly not judged.

A man called Charlie bounded up to me with the red chubby cheeks of a Punch and Judy doll. He was very smiley and very nice and terribly keen about everything I said. He was also terribly keen to get a selfie. "It's great to see people bringing something to Hastings, it's good to be on the map, do you mind if I post this?". He said he was something important locally but I didn't really hear him because of the wind and I could tell I'd disappointed him a little by not reacting with more deference or appreciation. He started talking about how we really ought to do more for people who were struggling, and when I said we didn't really do anything like that he looked perplexed. I tried to explain that we weren't a fixing space and not a service and sometimes all people needed was a space for company where they could mutually ... and no ... I'd lost him ... he was looking at me like I'd stepped on his cat. "Look I've got to go to an event, guest of honour and all that, but I'd really like to learn more," then I watched the back of his overcoat hastily race away from me.

Hastings, the town, is a character in itself. It feels like an old military hero fallen on hard times. Grand, important, full of stories of battles but totally skint with holes in its pockets. The famous and phenomenal singer and pianist Liane Carroll calls her hometown "a drug town with a fishing problem". The permanent public living room there is run by some folks who call themselves "Hastings Commons". They created it out of an old furniture shop. It's really big, full of multi-coloured throws and big armchairs and very, very cosy. The Hastings Common folks are leading a quiet revolution. "Regeneration without gentrification". Jess Steele, who runs it, is a friend and hero of mine and she came down with her little yappy-type dog on a lead and told me I'd picked a spot that was basically a wind tunnel. The flaw in my activism on the pavements is that I'm never a local. Memo to self – ask local Camerados next time where to put my sofa.

WHAT THE HELL IS THIS?

I've been putting furniture on pavements and talking to strangers for a couple of years now and "sofa" I've not been arrested. Little furniture gag for you there.

I've had armchairs and occasional tables too. And rugs. And a standard lamp. After I've parked the van I normally sit down and read a newspaper. People come along and look at the furniture and say "What the hell is this?" and I look up and say "I don't know" as if I've just come across it too. So this way when they sit down they talk to me like I am just another person, not staff.

I've heard about people's wild swimming escapades; their military career; the day they influenced the President of the United States; their grief after losing their grandchild; their ideas to save the local steel works; their mother's curry recipe; their technique to burn hair from nostrils; their renditions of songs and their favourite jokes. These all really happened. And it was mutual too – they listened to me ramble on, they made me think and they kindly laughed at my crap jokes.

It's not strictly legal to put furniture on streets so I've met a lot of policemen and some security guards wearing stab vests too. Also met some people from the council with lanyards. Only a few times were they unfriendly, for the most part we had some grand conversations.

In Belfast we were a bit bold and just dumped a very large public living room in the middle of Donegal Street opposite the McDonald's and outside JD Sports. Officials from the council stood and watched us from across the road for ages. Then they wandered over and said: "We see what you're doing and it's great, we love it, stay as long as you like!" One security guard in Manchester led me away to see his manager, but during the time it took to get there he opened up to me about his sister being beaten up by her husband and his own struggle with depression. When we arrived he gave a glowing recommendation to his boss about what we were doing. To be honest, I hadn't really said a thing to him, he just talked his way into getting what it was all about.

I've collected these little pen-picture stories of people I met in the pavement public living rooms. You'll meet them in the chapters with the titles of the towns I've visited. I hope you'll enjoy just listening to our conversations, see what's going on in people's lives. I don't go into tons of detail because as you'd imagine with a short time spent chatting to strangers these were fleeting chance encounters and, though often things got deep, they are really nothing more than snatches and dispatches from people's lives. That is what it was like on the street and it was all the more compelling. Have you ever looked at a city landscape at night and wondered what stories lay behind the lights in all those windows? Well, I was lucky enough to get just a glimpse.

I hope you connect with them. The relationship I'm really after here is not the one I struck up on the street but the one you get with them from reading these stories. I'm sure things in common will spring up for you, you'll see some of yourself here, or a friend or relative perhaps. If you're reading this and you sometimes feel alone, I want you to hear about these people and realise you're not. People are living lives that are sometimes rosy and sometimes stormy in streets up and down the land just like you. These lives may be deemed ordinary but I hope you agree many, if not all, are in their own way totally extraordinary.

A REALLY OBVIOUS IDEA TO CHANGE THE GODDAMN WORLD

There is, however, more to the sofas. Behind it lies a global movement that is slowly growing. This pavement stuff I'm doing is just a sideshow raising awareness of the main attraction.

The real work happens in communities around the world. They do this really obvious thing, but for some reason people think that it's totally radical, which it isn't but hey.

It's this thing called a "public living room" and they're not generally on the streets. They are in hospitals, libraries, parks, bandstands, cafés and community centres. There was once one in a prison, one on a canal boat and there still is one down by a beach. There are currently 250 in neighbourhoods across the UK, USA, Australia, New Zealand, and our first one in Africa is in Sierra Leone – that's the one on the beach – in Freetown.

This is the real story. You will spot some pictures of these public living rooms, just like they pop up in neighbourhoods they'll surprise you by appearing randomly at the end of chapters to surprise and inspire you! Some open every day, some once a week or once a month, some pop up now and again, some for a couple of hours on a Saturday morning. Some are created as part of people's job and some just happen because their creators give a damn about people in their neighbourhood. They are carried out by Camerados, a worldwide movement that isn't hitting the headlines and doesn't particularly want to, it just fumbles along with the grain of people's lives. They do things when it feels right, not out of guilt or compulsion, and they figure stuff out person by person, neighbourhood by neighbourhood. They're a bit crap and fine with it, they want to create spaces that aren't driven by perfection, by agendas, by religion, by a political ideology and the only shared condition among them is being human and being together. I started it in my bedroom nine years ago.

If you wanna find out about it google us, I'm not here to sell you it because this book is not about that. This book is just a collection of stories from towns where I've plonked a sofa on the pavement. And it is also a collection of ideas.

So I've organised it into two different kinds of chapters. Chapters named after the towns where I've plonked a sofa on the street and chapters with the ideas. These ideas are sometimes surprising, a little challenging maybe, they might even make you grip your chin, narrow your eyes, push your glasses up your nose (if you don't wear glasses just do the action with your finger) and say "Hmmm very interesting that Maff!" in a whiny voice like you're being really nerdy. Or they might make you throw a rubber plant out of the window because you're THAT cross. Rubber plant cross. Either way, these are ideas which are, I think, quite interesting, a bit confounding, and might spark something in you. They have arisen from all our years of mistakes and lessons learnt developing the Camerados movement and public living rooms. Some of the ideas came from long before that too ...

I've spent 30 years working in and around people with fairly shitty lives sometimes in very traditional and institutional settings, sometimes not. Sometimes as CEO of a charity or an adviser to the UK government wearing a suit and having business lunches that featured a lot of Halloumi. Sometimes with bin bags tied around my hands lifting mounds of human faeces out of toilets in homeless shelters. I have learnt a lot about people and the places that try to help them. I put all of that into creating Camerados. You have some profound conversations when you run places for people in times of crisis. Either they feel like they couldn't fall any lower, or they are thinking of bringing it to an end, and this is when you hear about what truly matters to people. It turns out that it isn't housing or sorting their money out, which is a shame since that was pretty much all we did in the services I worked in for twenty years. Turns out what mattered was this blindingly obvious thing. I think it can really help you too. How? I'll come to that, but first let's go to Birmingham.

BIRMINGHAM

DRUID'S HEATH

Victor is a big fella in a red chequered lumberjack shirt, baseball cap, probably late sixties. He was using a metal walking stick to make his way up the pavement towards us. He looked in a lot of pain. However, as soon as we started talking about Elvis, the crutch was discarded and he gave an impromptu performance of "Let's twist again, like you did last summer" complete with singing and twisting dance moves.

I tell him that this song was Chubby Checker and he obviously doesn't know his Elvis. He throws me a look and the temperature drops. Other locals wink at me and lean forward to see what happens next. At this point it becomes clear that I've made perhaps the biggest mistake in the whole of the West Midlands that Tuesday. Victor proceeds to tell me why. He knows Elvis. He has MET Elvis, and in honour of this momentous occasion Victor has, by the sounds of it, one of the largest collections of Elvis memorabilia outside of Gracelands. In his Birmingham council house he has a huge number of old '78s of The King. He has a signed photo of Elvis and Mohammad Ali together. He has portraits painted of Elvis. An extensive library on Elvis. His dog is called Priscilla. I made the last bit up.

"So you know who Elvis is then?" I remark. "Never heard of the fella," he says and we all crease up. I ask him if he can do the Elvis thing with his legs but he wags his crutches and tells me that's not happening anymore. His infirmity is the result of his second near-fatal motorbike accident – described to me in great, gruesome detail – but he was chuffed to tell me that this did not stop him making the bus so he can cross town and get to Iceland once a week, which is where he is going now. It turns out that Iceland, (the supermarket, not the small island nation in the north Atlantic), offers a 10% discount on Tuesdays for the over 55s. So Victor painfully flogs it up the street on his crutches every week and catches

13

three – yes three – separate buses to get there and get his 10% discount. I mull this over in my head and decide that probably works out at around twenty pence off a bag of fish fingers. "Times are tough and Iceland wants to give us a hand," he says, as if he knew them personally. As he walks off to catch his bus, I can't help wishing he'd flog some of that Elvis stuff and not have to trek for discounts, but then you can't listen to a fish finger, you can't love it in the same way I suppose. Well you can but it would be weird.

Jeff has been sitting watching all this with a broad smile on his face. He turned up as soon as our sofa legs hit the street and is loving the vibe. When the pet food shop told us to move from outside their shop front (we were concealing the vinyl signs on their windows offering spectacular discounts on their rabbit food), it was Jeff who had the bright idea of plonking down outside the "Hong Kong House" Chinese takeaway. As he sensibly observed, they don't open till 5pm so we wouldn't be in anybody's way. Jeff wears a bright yellow hoodie and looks a bit like the big fella in *The Full Monty* who wraps himself in cling film. I don't mention this to Jeff cos that might sound a bit odd.

Jeff has offered everyone in the public living room the opportunity to get as many elephants as we want. "Erm what, sorry?" He has connections in Thailand, he goes there for half the year. He could get me up to six elephants apparently, though they eat a lot, he tells us, "Cost a fortune". Water buffalo is another option. Still pretty rough on the tonnage of food front though. As a group of strangers sat there in the public living room outside a Chinese takeaway, we seem to somehow collectively decide in that moment, without group discussion, to entertain Jeff's retail opportunity rather than make fun of him. I am quite proud of us for that. We ruminate on the question of where exactly we'd put the elephants or water buffalo in our houses – a mix of terraced and semi-detached – and how we'd walk them daily. "And don't forget the food bill," Jeff reminds us, as if we'd forgotten. The food bill was obviously my main sticking point for having elephants and water buffalo in my house. Jeff says he'd have more space probably because he lives alone. We chat further and it turns out Jeff's quite lonely when he's not in Thailand. The good news is that he loves a men's walking group which goes by the canals in Birmingham regularly. He says it keeps him sane. I mention the elephants and he says, "Well, OK

I'm obviously not THAT sane." We must've talked to Jeff for about three hours. Lovely fella.

Walter is probably in his thirties but the deathly white, creased up, un-shaven face says decades older. He professes with great vigour his love of horror movies, especially the gruesome ones. He grunts out big laughs as he says this, probably amused by our grimacing faces. He likes to shock, it gets a reaction. He helped us carry the sofas back into the van and we had a good laugh, despite his trousers being wet and soiled from urine and his black teeth hurting him like hell. I ventured the possibility to him that his teeth hurt on account of the eight sugars he requested in his tea when we did a drinks run earlier. I regret my insensitivity instantly but, more worryingly, Walter didn't even blink twice at my crass comment. He seems to just wander about the place most of the day and nobody wants anything to do with him. He goes in and out of shops making requests for this and that but it seems more a desire for conversation than that he really wants anything. Especially as he's just spent half an hour in the pet shop and he doesn't have any pets. I was worried about him carrying all our furniture because he had painfully thin limbs and the wingback arm-chairs aren't that light. He struggled on and was loving helping us. He kept saying, "I lifted that" and "It's a good job I'm here eh?!" My interminable fixing brain wanted to get him another highly sugary brew to say thanks but he'd wandered off to his next appointment. His appointment with nobody and nothing.

CARDIFF

Wahiba is holding a Starbucks takeaway cup and so is her friend, their black and brown Hijabs framing their faces and somehow accentuating and amplifying their wide eyes and happy, beaming smiles. "If I have daughters," Wahiba says, "I want them to know their mother was adventurous and that I travelled from Morocco to Wales to study!" Her friend fervently agrees. "People are lovely here but they don't really make friends with us. We end up just knowing other Arabic people."

As if to prove her point, we were joined a little while later by a young man from Yemen who chatted to them for a while about their shared experience of student life. Then a man sat down who told us he was a barber from Kurdistan. He had taught himself how to cut hair via YouTube videos for two years then went for a job in a salon pretending to have lots of experience. We all sat open mouthed at his audacity. Wahiba and I fired lots of questions at him "No, no, it was fine," he reassured our disbelieving faces, "it went well. The cuts, they weren't difficult, I'm still there, it's been a few years now," he said proudly. He then showed us videos how he burns the hair off his customers' ears & puts wax up their nostrils. We all made groaning and screeching noises as we watched. The two girls kept creasing up in laughter. "This isn't my usual YouTube channel," Wahiba remarks. "Oh no that man has the hairiest nostrils I've ever seen!" Cue more howling and hiding behind their hands.

After they left I was on my own for a bit. A group of young men suddenly emerged from the library opposite and took over the whole space. They were all young, black and wearing heavy quilted jackets. They just wanted to hang and most of them weren't the talkative type. One of them though was more forthcoming. He told me they were from an area of Cardiff called Butetown but had come into the city centre to study in the library.

17

After a few games of Connect Four he talked some more. "I don't like where I live," he said suddenly as we lined up for our next game, "too much violence. We come here to avoid the gangs." His friends nodded. After a while they said their studies beckoned and wandered back into the library.

I was chatting to Paul for about an hour when he suddenly says, "Look Maff, I'm basically your classic nightmare in the town centre on a Saturday night." Paul is naked to the waist, wearing grey jogging bottoms and filthy trainers, carries a Tesco plastic bag full of something, half of one of his ears has been bitten off and his teeth are black. He is great company, smiling at everything everyone says, waving enthusiastically at passers by and seemingly chuffed to bits to be in our weird gang on the pavement sofas. "What do you mean?" I ask. "You seem a lovely fella to me." "Nah Maff I'm not gonna lie to you I'm a right crazy bastard man, especially on a Saturday night. Although," he carries on, "I turned a bit of a corner recently." He looks thoughtful and tells his tale.

"I went bounding into the Night Shelter a few weeks ago, I was really up and excited to see everyone. I shouted at John behind the desk and I guess I was a bit over the top like, you know a bit loud maybe, and he told me to quiet down. But I didn't, I misread the situation and thought John was being sarky or something so I kept shouting jokes and teasing him and before I knew it John chucked me out, he said I was upsetting folk in the queue and I couldn't have a bed that night. I walked out really angry with myself. I wandered down the street shouting harsh words to myself for being stupid when I heard laughter from some people outside a pub off to my right. I convinced myself they were laughing at me so I goes over there, and you know, well Maff not gonna lie to you but things got out of hand pretty quickly. A blue light came round the corner and I knew how the night would play out: a gang of coppers, an assault charge, some criminal damage, someone gets hurt, hospital maybe, ambulances, I'd end up in the cells, court proceedings ... all the rest. I knew it was coming. Except that night it didn't. It was the wildest thing that happened next." We all leaned in, hanging on Paul's every word.

"This policeman walks towards me and do you know what he does?" We shook our heads. "He goes: 'Alrigh' Paul what's got you all in a Tizzy now then?' Then he throws open his arms and says 'Come here and give us a cuddle!". Well that stops me in my tracks!" Paul is looking at us as aghast as he had been in the story. "He didn't have to say that, did he? Wasn't that nice of the police fella? It calmed me right down, it did. And after that things went OK. And not being funny but I haven't caused trouble for weeks now cos, well you see, I don't wanna let him down."

AND NOW ... THE MEANING OF LIFE

The idea that it's not that complicated

Well this is a nice bonus. I bet you never thought when you bought this book that contained inside it would be the meaning of life. That's nice then.

In fact it's all done and dusted in this one chapter. Honestly, the amount of time people have spent trying to figure it out, all those philosophers banging on about it across millennia, the centuries of religious leaders praying about it ... all the blood and tears by generations of artists ... . those poor folk bless them, they really overcooked it. You'll be done in a few pages.

Well actually, two words. It's hardly a mystery since I used them for the title of this book, but let me get you to do some work to find the path that leads there.

In my time before Camerados I spent many years running places that really hoped to turn people's lives away from chaos and towards some kind of fulfilling life. More often than not we did not achieve that change. I've rehoused thousands of people, finding them a room in a shared house or a one bedroom flat. It was often miles and miles from anyone they knew and anyone they had a connection with, and we left them to stare at blank walls and expected it to transform their life. We might have got them a shelf-stacking job in ASDA and a qualification too. None of this was in any way related to what could reignite the pilot light that had gone out inside them and all of it would end up ultimately reasserting that they were basically worthless. I never once asked these people before they departed our hostels or refuges whether they had the stuff that gave their life meaning. Never mentioned it once.

We spent years overcomplicating the whole thing. We ran services suffocating in paper like Robert De Niro's character in the movie *Brazil*. Forms to fill in, needs and risk assessments, outcome stars, KPIs, measuring the life trials of people like we were laying pipe or building a road, not dealing with human beings.

Yet surrounded by this dizzying complexity, it occurred to me that really when you stripped all that away weren't we just trying to increase the frequency of happy days and decrease the rubbish ones? Aren't all of us doing that in our life? When we lie on our deathbeds isn't that a pretty fundamental abacus on which to judge a decent life? Did we have more happy days than unhappy ones?

So that led me to desperately want to know what were the essential ingredients in creating happy days so that we could manufacture more of them. To find out, I've been doing my own live research! Wherever I go to speak to people I have asked them to do a little exercise with me. I'm going to ask you to do this now. The only problem is it involves closing your eyes which makes reading this book a bit tough ... so maybe read it first then do it, yes? Cheers.

I ask people to close their eyes. I ask them to imagine they are sitting in a huge cinema alone, in the dark. On the screen comes a title, white on black. It is their name and underneath it says "The Movie". Amazingly, in this cinema they have given you a remote control and you get to control the film. I ask them to press and hold the fast forward button and race through the first 11 years of your life.

What can you see?

Ok stop. Take it in. Now press again and race through your teenage years. How was that? Good times? Bad times? Awkward times?

Now hold down that button and race through the rest of your life from 18 years old up until today. For some of you this may take a while (!) others not so much.

Ok. So there were some big moments and some tiny details I'm sure that leapt into your mind. Now I want you to move your finger over to the rewind button on the remote and go back to a day when you felt you were happy. It doesn't have to be the happiest day of your life, in fact it's best if you go to just an averagely happy day. A day when you probably thought to yourself, "this is what it's all about." Maybe you even said that out loud at the time. That day everything just came together and you felt content. Life was good. Now look around yourself on that day. Notice what is there.

What I do then is ask people to open their eyes and hopefully some of them will be brave enough to share where they were and what was going on.

I have asked that question in rooms full of people – from five to 1,000 – for about 12 years now. That's a lot of people, thousands I suppose. And the answers have been wonderful and varied, some action packed, some quiet. There's always someone who wants to share the location of their amazing holiday(!), somebody who forgets the "not the happiest day of your life" request and gushes tearfully about their wedding day or the birth of a child, very often people talk about being on a beach, having barbecues in the park, festivals, there's often a lot of nature. Would it surprise you if I told you that their answers only ever fall into two categories?

Isn't that amazing? People from all walks of life, all backgrounds, many countries even ... thousands of them ... and yet their happy days contained only two ingredients.

For around 80–90% of people their happy day involved spending time with other people. People they cared about. Loved ones, friends, people who mattered to them.

The remaining 10–20% were doing something they loved or were proud of doing. Climbing a mountain, finishing a marathon, performing at a concert, getting that job, being sober for a year.

After 12 years of asking this question to wildly varied audiences, my belief is that happy days consist of these two things: friends and purpose.

So let's not overcomplicate it. We fill our lives with all sorts of things that we think we need and we need to worry about. We make decisions based on those presumptions. In 30 years of working with people who have very shitty lives, like I said earlier, I don't recall the services I ran having a major focus on these two things. We covered the housing and money angles and maybe employment, which I guess is purpose of a kind, but all too often I was getting people work placements that funnily enough weren't really connected to their "purpose".

I should have spotted these two things without the "movie of your life" game. I had spent 20 years chatting to people on the cliff edge of life, toes dangling over the edge thinking is it worth sticking around because things had got so bad. Funnily enough they don't talk about housing much. Or money. If I'd taken more notice I would've realised that they always talk about the people they love or the things they are passionate about, that gives their life meaning and purpose.

So if friends and purpose create happy days and they also pop up when you're considering what makes life worth living, then when people go through a tough day or a tough time maybe we should bring them into the conversation. That is what the Camerados movement is aiming for.

So how do we get Friends and Purpose? Well you can't create a friend for someone or invent purpose easily overnight (anyone who has parented a teenager will attest to that last point, wonderful though my teenage boys are!). So all you can do is create the environment for that to occur. That environment doesn't just mean a physical space; it also means a "vibe". The physical space does some of the heavy lifting for you, but the vibe, the values, the silent contract we all sign up for when we are together in a certain way, this is created by people's behaviour in that space. The principles in a Camerados' public living room aim to help you do that.

I used to separate out the "purpose" bit. In the early days I thought we should put activities into the public living rooms, some music perhaps, or maybe a notice board directing people to great walking groups, choirs, colleges in the neighbourhood. Some public living rooms probably have those things but I hadn't realised that the purpose was happening already, right under my nose. When people look out for someone else and have their back, when they provide them with the gift of their own company, that alone is a mighty dose of purpose right there. So it turns out that you got both Friends and Purpose in one big caffeine hit just by sitting alongside someone else.

So there you have it folks. Friends and purpose. The meaning of life. Everything else is for the birds.

ALLOA

A policeman shows up. He's called Alan. As usual we don't have permission to be on the pavement with all our furniture so we're on edge a little. To be fair, we've chosen a very conspicuous spot right at the top of the high street outside a prominent charity shop in a little mini piazza.

PC Alan is young, a big lad, ginger hair protruding from his policeman's hat. He's really tooled up, handcuffs waving from his belt and a Hi-Viz jacket covering up what looks like Kevlar. He stands in front of us and lets out a big sigh.

"I'm on parking duty today," he says with a forlorn tone, whipping out a mini reporter's pad like it's a Star Trek communicator, and producing a pen from his lapel pocket to join it. "Yep that's right," he says loudly, "I used to have a soul!"

We collapse in laughter, he smiles and stays a while, perched on the end of one of the big armchairs just beside the litter bin. He's one of the most philosophical police officers I have met, talking about his town and the things he sees, people he meets. He reminds me of the story that took place on the Brooklyn Bridge in New York City. Some Camerados had made a mobile public living room out of balsa wood (a fold out backdrop of a fireplace, some fold out chairs, obligatory fairy lights) and they had been wheeling it around on a trolley across Manhattan and Brooklyn streets, subways, and now, bridges. They were scared when a police officer showed up – they saw the size of their gun and started to pack up in anticipation of trouble. Yet the same thing happened there as in Alloa. The cop asked them what they were doing, listened and then just sat down and joined in. Apparently the NYPD officer stayed for about an hour. The police are, after all, part of the community too and most likely joined the force to help that community. Perhaps this is why in all our time doing street activism it has never been a police officer that has moved us on, only private security guards.

Alloa is the main town in the county of Clackmannanshire, sandwiched between the more famous, more illustrious Stirling and Perth. That day I heard people refer to something called "The Clacks effect", a term used to describe what has happened to the hearts and minds of people who live there. I must confess, it gave me a chill. They say people have stopped creating things, stopped making new projects happen, because "why bother when you're only going to get your heart broken again". They say it's been like this since the 1990s. A brilliant local community worker and entrepreneur called Angela cites one story where a volunteer came along out of the blue one day, a woman in her fifties in dungarees with a workman's belt and a baseball cap. She picked up power tools and helped them completely decorate a room in an abandoned factory that they are trying to resurrect for community use. Upon leaving, Angela said: "Wow you have been amazing, thank you so much, see you again tomorrow?" "You won't," said the woman. "Why not?" Angela asked. "Well, I guess you're from Edinburgh. We see your kind all the time. It's nice of you. You come and try to change things. But it never works out and you leave again. I won't be hanging around to see that happen." That's the Clacks effect and legend has it the whole town suffers from it. I can't believe it's true because otherwise it's just too bleak. The town that gave up.

As the afternoon progressed, plenty of passersby confounded that theory in my mind by bringing bonhomie, cheeky gags and much laughter. They all thought we were mad but chatted to us anyway. Even the kids coming back from school stopped their scooters and shared their sweetie bags with us. A major argument broke out about cola bottles versus those sweets that look like fried eggs. I'm for cola bottles every time just saying. Behind all the comings and goings, a few of us noticed another story unfolding in the centre of town. A tall fella making his way from shop to shop, pub to pub, half staggering, half dancing across the street and behind us. He was what we call a "wanderer". On my travels I've encountered this phenomenon everywhere. Our towns and cities are full of wanderers. People without any purpose, perhaps between appointments with various key workers assigned to them, killing time by just wandering the streets, carrying around God Knows What in their head.

Always thought it perplexing how we make people dependent on a sea of key workers covering a myriad of different aspects of their life; we then make them meet them for 45 minute appointments each week, where the troubled and frantic contents of their worried minds are poked at and discussed, and then we leave them to wander around a pretty isolated world with these thoughts for the other remaining 12 hours of their day, expecting that all to work out OK. This fella seemed to talk to everyone then wander out and into the next place. He was hugely tall, very thin, dressed in jeans and a lumberjack shirt with wild hair and a straggling beard, like an elongated Yosemite Sam. We overheard him a little from a distance, and it sounded like he was talking gibberish and people were being kind but laughing to each other as he walked off. Eventually he wandered up to us, his bulking, lumbering frame blocking out the sun as he peered down at our little set up. A pause. A silence. He took it all in. Then he threw open his arms, his eyes lit up and he said:

"I LOVE THIS!"

The collection of random folk sat around us couldn't help but let out a little cheer and he sat down on one of the sofas. To our surprise this larger than life character fell mute. He didn't say another word, he just studied everyone and listened to our conversation. Like with his other interactions around town, he didn't hang around for long and up he leapt and strode off towards another pub. As we watched his back pass through the traffic one of our group said, "For that 10 minutes I think he felt normal." I don't know exactly what he meant – I'm not a big fan of the term "normal" – but I took it to mean something more like "accepted".

I returned from a biscuit-buying mission at the shops to find that a fella wearing a flat cap had joined us and was perpetually yanking back two large, blonde, regal Afghan hounds. Their snouts were hunting down the backs of our chairs for biscuits. The owner's name is Colin and he tells me that his wife died of cancer earlier that year and if it wasn't for the two dogs he wouldn't get out of bed in the morning. He didn't see the point in living, he tells us matter-of-factly. However, every morning the dogs grab hold of his pyjama bottoms and pull him out of the bed and onto the floor.

He reluctantly gets up and dressed because he knows he has to take them for their walks. On these walks he meets people, people who love his dogs and ask them about them.

Colin stayed for well over an hour telling me his incredibly varied life story – bus conductor, karate teacher, working in a power station – I couldn't believe the variety of jobs so asked him in detail about each one showing, in the process, my ignorance of anything sporty or practical, much to Colin's amusement. There seemed to be no connection between Colin's jobs at all; it was just the meandering mad happenstance that occurs when sometimes you follow the money, sometimes a lover, sometimes just plain geography.

Then a passerby said he should show the dogs at Crufts, the famous dog show, because they are so beautiful, whereupon Colin announces that he had indeed competed at Crufts for many years! We all cheered at this news and other people passing by sat down to listen to his tales of this mythical dog show. He told us about preening owners, misbehaving dogs, adventures in dog agility rounds and TV celebrities handing out awards. The mention of Peter Purves drew sighs and nods from those of us above a certain age who remember ancient children's television. All this magic had stopped though when his wife died, Colin told us. We all sat in silence with him, and a stranger, a professional looking woman in her thirties, leant across and gave his arm a squeeze.

When he got up to leave I rarely felt sincerity like it as he fixed me with a steely glare, grabbed my hands with his own rough pair and said, "I've so enjoyed our conversation." Then as he looked around at the public living room and the people in it he said a sentence I've heard more times than any other sentence on my travels:

"We need more of these."

A PUBLIC LIVING ROOM

Relax, share, laugh, look out for each other.

Be a Camerado.

5 PRINCIPLES

Public living rooms
from around the world
Baltimore
U.S.A.

BETTER THAN LASAGNE

The idea the we don't always do what people really need in a crisis

Can it be possible that there is something better than Lasagne? Well yes, amazing but true. Read on ...

There is another reason I wrote this book. The world needs the power of connection right now. More than ever in its history. Ok Mr Movie Trailer Man, enough of the melodrama, what do you mean? Well, put it this way, we need this more than we need Lasagne. And I love Lasagne.

The pavements I visit are usually in towns and neighbourhoods that are having a tough time. The Government data tell us they are in the top percentiles for income deprivation[1] so I guessed they'd be hit the hardest by this thing people are calling a "cost of living crisis". I started doing it because of the way everyone was reacting to this "crisis". It was the same response we make when any sort of crisis hits: everybody starts making Lasagne.

We also start collecting blankets. I'm not sure if anyone specifically asked for Lasagne and blankets but that's what turns up. It's the standard community response. Fair enough I suppose, maybe this is a very useful and also a lovely thing to do. I'm pretty sure it is. However, it really felt like people needed reminding that there's something far worse than food poverty, which makes you hungry, or fuel poverty, which makes you cold, and that is a poverty of connection, which makes you lose the will to live. It is the thing that matters most to people.

[1] *Exploring local income deprivation: A detailed picture of disparities within Engl[...] neighbourhood level.*

33

I used to have a death every 16 days in the homeless hostels I ran and when I investigated all the deaths, isolation was at the root of all of them. When times are hard we push everyone away, either through shame, pride, guilt, embarrassment, whatever, we just want to be alone. Which is ironic because it's the opposite of what will really pull us through our tough times. As I said earlier, people on the cliff edge of life are thinking only about the other people in their life, people with whom they have a connection. That's what matters to them most. This is what they will miss, what they crave, what keeps them on the right side of that cliff; and Lasagne, though lovely, isn't going to cut it.

However, connection takes time and effort and on top of that it has been having a hard time recently. The worst in fact.

This thing that is our biggest tool for getting through tough times became globally illegal in 2020. The pandemic told us to all stop doing it, stop coming together and physically being together. That started alarm bells for me. Will this disconnection become habitual? Then immediately after the pandemic we were hit by an economic crisis so now the cost of living stops people from getting together even if they wanted to – they can't afford to meet up. Then you add to this a whole stormfront of divisive issues pulling us apart: culture wars, actual wars, climate crisis (just stop for a second and take those three things in for a bit … . nope keep thinking about them … because each one is massive, the last one being the most massive and planet-consuming of all of course). Then, with perfect timing and to the great delight of the world's media, we have the most polarised time in politics in living memory. Anybody hoping that the world will bring to the fore the political leaders we need to galvanise us to solve these problems, well we seem to be instead electing leaders who stoke division and ignite violence, not everywhere, but in the places with the most people and the most power. It feels like there's never been a time, certainly while I've been alive, where division has been so prevalent and hard times so pervasive. All of which creates disconnection and isolation.

Sheesh. Time to bust open the custard creams cos this is depressing! Don't worry folks, it's actually a call to arms. Except don't take up arms, that would be bad, just put the kettle on. (If you're reading this in a country other than Britain that just means sit back and get some perspective. With a hot drink!)

We have to create these no-agenda places so we can stop screaming and shouting at each other and instead have each other's backs. If we all did this, neighbourhood by neighbourhood then we'd knit together a fabric that could change a lot of this, ground up, street by street.

It's not the whole answer to everything but it's a little thing that is needed to make the whole machine work (there's probably a metaphor needed here involving tiny little mechanisms inside powerful car engines but I'm about as practical as Gouda cheese so don't expect me to find that for you). Of course we need institutions and services and clinics but if they don't have the human element they ultimately fail in their endeavour. I find myself saying this a lot but: the only thing complex, messy and intricate enough to understand the complexity, messiness and intricacies of a human being is ... .

... another human being.

All our problems, our hang ups, our histories, every one different, every one triggered by something different, the only thing able to respond well to all of that is another messed up human. Find a way for humans to see each other as human, and we'll stop screaming, shouting and fighting and everyone will get along a bit better.

And if we don't? If we burn up in space through our own climate stupidity or blow ourselves to bits in our inexorable desire for war, well at least this way we'll have a bit of company.

SCARBOROUGH

The bay in Scarborough is beautiful, a perfect curve of surf nudging up against a picturesque little marina of fishing boats and pleasure cruisers, an arc of amusement arcades, a beach full of dog walkers and joggers and looking over the whole scene is a terrifying gothic hotel on the cliffs, dimly lit in the evening light as if deliberately concealing a murderer for an Agatha Christie detective to pursue among its labyrinthine corridors. I wandered around the streets and hills in this striking scene for hours that evening because I needed to process all the stories I'd heard on the streets that day. I had been so busy, I guess 200 hundred people had sat down. One person whose story and whole demeanour had stayed with me was Dennis.

Dennis had nestled into the wingback armchair as if he was at home. A lovely fella in his late sixties with big square steel-framed glasses, grey wavy hair and a gravelly, deep voice. He seemed to need company more than most. He was unshaven, a bit unkempt but it didn't seem like he was short of money; he was just not taking as good care of himself as perhaps he had done in the past. A possible reason revealed itself as we talked about shopping and the town centre. He used to come to the café over the road with his wife. He lost Eileen some years ago, she was only 52, and the phone had rung at work to tell him to come home. He didn't understand, his brain didn't take it in until he saw the ambulance outside his house and even then he went into full denial. She was on the floor of the living room, brain aneurysm, but he didn't believe it. He just carried on wandering around the house, making a cup of tea, putting the dinner on. The ambulance crew called for backup and a female police officer turned up, put the kettle on and stayed with him until he finally took it in – he sobbed for hours with her.

He talks to Eileen still. When he gets in the door he says "I'm home love" every single day. He started doing it cos he'd forget she wasn't there but now it's just something he does to feel close to her. He says they chat endlessly even though he knows it's in his head. But then he also believes in the supernatural. Shockingly, he reveals that he lost his grandchild recently. He didn't say how but she had been a toddler, I guessed maybe three or four years old. He said one day something happened which unnerved him but also brought him a huge amount of comfort. He visited his grandchild's grave and planted a little children's windmill by her headstone. Before leaving he told her to make it spin for her grandad and it did, straight away. It spun round and round. He watched it spin with tears in his eyes, not wanting to leave. He walked off after it had stopped but then looked back and he swears it started spinning again, just for him. Dennis can see he has an audience now for his story, a couple of women with shopping bags sat on the sofa opposite, a young studious-looking man on the armchair, a couple of guys in suits sat awkwardly on the bean bags, we're all just letting him talk. He smiles at us. "Go home and tell your loved ones that you love them," he says. "Do it every day." We all nod in silence then one of the suits says, "I promise Dennis," and one of the women shoppers echoes the same.

It was the day of a teacher's strike and the strikers were out in force in the street with flags, leaflets, petitions and oddly enough, sweets and chocolates for passersby. They all crowded around the public living room though, when something joyful happened. A young girl had been striding up and down the street all morning. She had thick-rimmed glasses, dark bob, purple T-shirt and lycra leggings and she had Down syndrome. She was moving her head from side to side, listening to music through enormous headphones. She sat down on a beanbag on the edge of our semicircle of furniture. I asked her what she was listening to. "'The Greatest Showman," she said. She then told us she was a really great singer herself. I asked her to give us a tune. At this point she clicked her music onto the track she wanted to sing along with and began. I don't think she realised we couldn't hear the music but she sang loudly along with it all the same. As she sang she signed along using Makaton so it felt like a glorious dance performance too. She was incredibly expressive and threw her heart and soul into the words. A crowd wandered towards us and stood all around her watching. She had her eyes closed for most of her song so when she opened them she was taken aback to see all of us there in front of her, and even more so when we erupted into applause and cheers. She didn't smile, she just stopped her music, packed away her headphones, looked up at us and said, very matter of factly, "I love my life." Then she left, at speed, down the street. We all stood and gaped, looking at each other exchanging looks that said: "Did that just happen?"

David was in his mid-thirties and we struck up a conversation when I admired his brown leather jacket. He was a snappy dresser, had a kind round face, bushy hair and a demeanour that seemed to be perpetually smiling. He had intended to leave Scarborough when he was 19, he told me, as he had a place at one of the top drama schools in London. It was his dream to be an actor. However, a freak incident outside a pub the Friday night before the weekend that he was due to leave changed his life forever. A man stabbed him in the head with an axe. He didn't know the guy but he mistook David for someone else. And was drunk. How he had an axe or the story behind the case of mistaken identity was never explained. David turned his head to one side and lifted his busy hair and I saw the scar. It was very long and very wide and all across one side of his head. He had been in hospital for a long time then spent most of his twenties suffering from depression, extremely low confidence and unable to leave the house. He never made it to London or drama school, nothing much had gone right for him since.

However, he gets up every day now and he looks for the positive about still being alive. He busies himself with numerous volunteering activities – helping other people has become his thing. He keeps busy. He works in a charity shop. He was particularly pleased today because he'd just been in a little boutique where they sell crystals and alternative medicines and the woman working there told him he had a beautiful aura! She talked to him for ages and said that he really did have a lovely personality. "I do, I think," he said, "it was really nice for her to notice and to tell me!" He beamed as if he'd won a cash prize.

When I was packing the furniture away – helped by two passing Mormons, as it happened – I noticed a few of my sofa companions from that day had moved their conversations to a nearby café. There was Dennis in the window with one of the women shoppers and they were hooting with laughter.

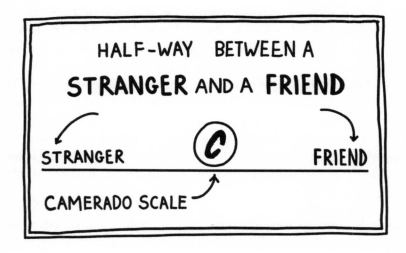

"I'M NOT YOUR FRIEND, I'M YOUR CAMERADO"

The idea that maybe a "friend" isn't always what you need

This is the point you find out you've bought a book with a faulty title. When I say to people that the answer to everything is "Friends and Purpose" I do so with an awareness that actually the first word "Friends" isn't entirely right. Sorry to break that to you after you've bought the book. What I really want to say is "Connection" but there's something weirdly clinical about saying "Connection and Purpose". It's not something you say in the course of daily conversation and so it stands out, like a "term" a professional might say. Whereas everyone can understand what a friend is. Of course there are many kinds of friends too, many gradations, depths, and so it's a word that can handle a little bit of imprecise use, I'm hoping. In our work building this movement, we learnt that it can also be a little misleading and plain wrong though, for a guy called Wayne anyhow. He came along and rocked our world. He made us realise that instead of "Friends and Purpose" it could really just be that we need a "Camerado".

The name "Camerados" comes from a poem by one of my favourite poets Walt Whitman. He wrote a poem called "Song for the Open Road" where he says that on the open road of life more important than money, more important than food, you need a Camerado alongside you.

> Camerado, I give you my hand!
> I give you my love more precious than money,
> I give you myself before preaching or law;

41

Will you give me yourself? will you come travel with me?
Shall we stick by each other as long as we live?

My wife, Ruth, and I had that read at our wedding and Camerado became a word I used when addressing pals in emails. Two of those pals ran a design agency, and as a favour to me, they used their scientific brand building framework to find a name for this venture of mine ... we went to the pub. After the first pint they told me I had already named this thing and it was "Camerados", because that's what I called them in all my emails. I hadn't realised. And so it became the name of this new community interest company. When others got on board with me it found its way onto business cards and email signatures and I started to have the confidence to use it. However, that changed, like most things in our movement, when people in communities got a hold of it. One fella in particular, called Wayne.

When we overheard Wayne use the word "camerado" as a noun, not a proper noun, a name, as we had been using it, he gave it a meaning.

Wayne is six foot four or more, bald, and could, on a bad day, cut quite a menacing figure. Yet he can be the loveliest, sweetest guy. At 14 he shoplifted as a dare (and a desire to fit in with his mate) and this put him in the youth detention centre where the other lads introduced him to drugs. Fast forward 30 years of intermittent prison time for drug-related offences and he wandered into the Camerados public living room in Blackpool. Wayne was at a crossroads of his life. Something in our public living room had bitten him, given him ideas. He started sitting outside the offices of Blackpool council a few times a week with cupcakes. He'd buy them with his benefit cheque and hand them to office workers who looked stressed on their way to work. No reason, just to cheer them up.

He also bought a bubble gun and on weekends he'd walk around the town leaving trails of bubbles for kids to play with behind him as he walked. It was a conversation starter, a way to connect to people and also just something to bring a bit of fun to people's day. This was a man who had a sufficiently long criminal record you could imagine that the police were always watching. Once, when I knew him, he was tying his shoelace beside a car when its alarm went off and the nearby police nicked him and put him in the cells overnight.

One day in the public living room we overheard Wayne say to someone:

"Listen pal I'm not your friend but I'm your camerado, I've got your back OK?"

We were fascinated by this so we bought him a cuppa and asked him "What does 'I'm your camerado' mean?" Like I said, at this point it was just our company name. Wayne looked at us like we were mad and as if we should know. Out of his mouth came a sentence fully formed and perfect in every sense: "A camerado is halfway between a stranger and a friend."

Boom! We asked him why couldn't the fella just be your friend, being as surely a friend is a good thing. At this Wayne blew air out of his mouth. "Ah well ... a friend is a bit heavy, you know, you have an obligation to your friends, you've got to sort them out when they're in trouble. Fix everything for them. It's quite a lot of pressure. Plus they know all your other friends so there's history there, baggage. It's a big deal. What I want is somebody alongside me for 10 minutes or half an hour or whatever who has my back and I have theirs ... no questions, no answers, no pressure, just a camerado."

And that was that. Thank you Wayne. We all need someone halfway between a stranger and a friend – connection is enough.

We then knew that the purpose of our movement was to create as many Camerados in the world as possible. People just looking out for each other who weren't necessarily friends. Strangers who gave a damn and had your back but didn't have to fix you. It fit perfectly with the "no solution revolution" that we were trying to bring about (see future chapter!), but Wayne framed it perfectly for us, it was part of the whole relationship. It was a bit of a drag at first because we had to change the name of our company at Companies House to reflect Wayne's vision! How could we be called "Camerados" if that's what we called each other? So we changed the company to "Association of Camerados" as we now realised that our job was to support the movement of people out there and grow them in number.

Wayne had hit upon something. It was what I'd heard called a "weak tie" by smart people who study how society works. I actually really dislike that term because "weak tie" sounds less important than a "strong tie" but it's a descriptor for the kind of relationship that sometimes exists and which can have surprisingly big impact.

I heard a brilliant story about such a thing on the world's favourite podcast *This American Life* [2] some years back, about a woman called Giulietta Carrelli. She had something called "Schizoaffective disorder" and ran a café in San Francisco called "The Trouble Coffee and Coconut Club". I won't rob you of the beautiful storytelling, you must listen yourself (footnote below), but the part that interested me about Giulietta's story was that her "disorder" meant she didn't always know where she was and she relied on strangers to get her home. She would have out-of-body experiences, she would hear voices and feel like perhaps she "didn't exist". So she always took the same route to the café. She befriended people along the route, like city workers digging up the road. She always wore the exact same thing – crop top, head scarves – and covered herself in distinctive tattoos. This way people would recognise her. So when she had an episode they'd know who she was, what was going on and where she had to go. She had built up her own support workers who were strangers to help her cope with her condition and keep her safe. They weren't family, they weren't friends, really they weren't strangers, I'd call them Camerados – as Wayne said "halfway between a stranger and a friend".

These weak ties were life saving for Giulietta. Imagine if we all had them as just part of our day? They are sadly rare in some communities, so when they happen it's something of a miracle for some people.

Have you ever sat on a bus or a train and struck up a conversation with the person next to you whereby you both suddenly share more than you might do with a friend or family member? Without even knowing their name? You say goodbye but feel a little like you had something a bit special just happen there. How great was it not to have any pressure about the things you say going any further or going back to any mutual acquaintances? Or that this person was going to suddenly lecture you?

That's being a camerado and it turns out we need them.

---

2   *No place Like Home*, episode 520, https://www.thisamericanlife.org/520/transcript

It was such a fascinating discovery to me that this thing that I felt was the big goal in all my social interactions – to find the great friend, the deep intense relationship – was perhaps not the only goal my life needed. Any assumption I had that less intense relationships were in some way inferior was incorrect. Those light, little connections in my day turned out to be so much more key that I realised. And if we could blow that up to a community and even a society, well now we're into some serious changing the world shit!

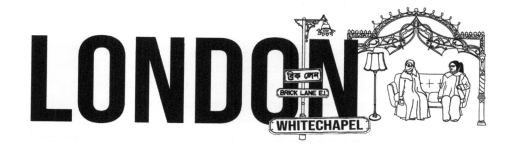

LONDON

Asok is an academic from Bangladesh and passing by our sofa, armchairs and chatter on the street in Whitechapel he stopped and stared at us with a quizzical expression. Conversation slightly fizzled out as we became aware of him glowering at us. He spoke, "What are you trying to reduce or increase by doing this?" he said. He looked concerned.

We started chatting and we discovered Asok's mind believed that everything, every project at least, must be trying to increase or reduce a commodity, an activity, and achieve a beneficial outcome, of some sort. We had a great disagreement, he was a fascinating fella and our discussion went back and forth about the human reflex towards outcomes, its necessity or its pointlessness, as he stood over us on the street, a short man with neat hair and dressed in a brown suit and tie that is somehow both smart and a bit dishevelled because it's just what he wears everyday.

Asok became delighted by the idea of there being a space that did not require an outcome or seek one. The idea that the sole purpose was to connect with another human, be alongside, not be alone, and see what happens. "This is new, it's radical, I've not seen it before." I disagreed and said that he probably has seen it before, many times, and we didn't feel it was radical at all because if we accept simple human connection as radical and innovative then surely we're all in trouble. He agreed this ought to be commonplace, and indeed it is completely understood by indigenous peoples who have always found that answers lie in community and hold dear the traditions around that. I punched the air in agreement at this, warming readily to the theme that western civilisation had abandoned this tradition in favour of an obsession with hierarchy and a social Darwinist view where some people are better than others. Asok was nodding, thinking, chewing it over in his head, "I know all this already," he said with

47

a glint in his eye behind his spectacles " ... but thanks for the reminder today." I realised I'd done that thing of talking for all of us, I do that when I get excited, so I apologised for appearing lecturing and he kindly shook his head and said it was OK. I offered him a cup of tea as I said it felt like we had at least another 12 hours to go on this discussion(!) but sadly he had to be somewhere. He had waved goodbye and walked off down the busy street before trotting back and raising his voice above the sounds of the traffic. "Just one more thing," we turned to look up at him " ... this no agenda approach, you know, just community, just connection ... it does achieve something though ... I mean that's the point ultimately isn't it? ... it helps life work, it makes our days better ... that's an outcome is it not?" We locked eyes, we both smiled. "You've got me there," I said. He continued, "Yes, there's always an increase or a decrease of something," and he raised his finger to the sky and his eyebrows too. "You've defeated me," I said, smiling. "Don't worry," he said as he turned to go, "I won't tell anyone." He winked, I laughed, he wandered off into the blurred figures bundling down Whitechapel high street.

The East London mosque started its call to prayer fifty yards to our right. The soaring sound of one solitary human singing out into the streets bounces off the walls of newsagents, curry houses and cab offices that hug the A11, otherwise known as Whitechapel Road. This part of the world is famous for Jack the Ripper, The Kray twins, the East End slums that inspired William Booth to create The Salvation Army – where I worked for a while – and now the streets are teeming with small eateries and businesses belonging mostly to a busy, bustling Asian community. But suddenly people are crossing the road in great numbers, emerging from doorways of shops and businesses and walking with purpose across the street into the mosque, one of the largest in Western Europe, capable of holding 7,000 worshippers.

We sit on the pavement, on our sofas and watch them pass by, some serious, some smiling in our direction. Students from the nearby London Interdisciplinary School – a newly formed university I had only recently learnt about – are drawing phrases on the pavement with our coloured chalk, words like "Smile at a stranger" or "Give us a smile". I slightly wince at this because I'm far too over-sensitive about the infantilization of our work into greetings' card aphorisms to do with smiles and rainbows (see the chapter on Bad Kindness) but then I remind myself that these young people are engaged and interested, exploring their way through this and maybe I should pull my head out of my arse and join in. I grab some chalk.

Some others are playing Connect Four – a staple of the pavement public living room – and some are arguing, still grappling with the debate Asok gave us that morning.

One student is from South America, and is animated with her hands and arms while kneeling on the hard pavement in rainbow-striped trousers. She declares to a group of fellow students, "I think society starts at the end point of what it wants and then works back to what we should be doing to serve that. You're given your goal, what quantifies success, and then told the steps to get there. Sometimes those steps have numbers, sometimes they're fucking colour coded depending on your progress, the level of satisfaction that society has in achieving *their* goals even! I'm sick of it. I don't want to do it anymore. I'm not society's project. I want to explore my life and not know where I'm going and stop trying to count me and my life all the time!!"

Her friends call her naive but she sounds pretty magnificent to me. Made me think of something I used to say all the time. Stand up and be counted? No. Sit down and don't be counted. With a cup of tea and some biscuits. And a conversation.

THE NO SOLUTION REVOLUTION

The idea that we can often do more good by not setting out to achieve anything.

Was Asok right? Is this radical? To create a project that sets out to achieve nothing. Perhaps it is, but consider for a moment the opposite approach. Almost everything we do follows a rigid and irresistible law that an outcome must be achieved.

The "logic model" rules almost everything we do, from commerce to parenting. This is the model that arose over the last half of the twentieth century and says:

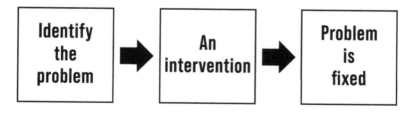

This progression is the way we project-manage everything. We are wedded to it, it is drilled into us if we want to be a successful, efficient manager of anything. It is unchallenged and blissfully accepted as Gospel if you want to live in a world that sells you stuff or fixes you. It makes sense if you're a car mechanic, a pilot or a surgeon, many walks of life I guess. The problem with the logic model is that it doesn't fit one really important thing …

… LIFE!

Life is never fixed. There's never an almighty "tick" when it's successfully sorted, nailed, done. When can any of us say that?

Our lives are more like a ball in a pinball machine going forward and back, up and down, good days, bad days, some of it in our control, some of it not, darting off in directions we didn't expect, and then we die. Conversations in public living rooms are much the same. Just without the death part. Hopefully.

The conversation meanders around many wonderfully pointless blind alleys and cul-de-sacs. A conversation about light fittings in your bathroom turns into an examination of masculinity, and then femininity, then somebody says "I've never really thought of that before" just before diving into a comparison between the films of Sigourney Weaver and those of Meryl Streep, leading to a chat about accents, an exploration on identity, "do any of us really come FROM anywhere?" Then football, why is Mbappe being left out of the squad this week? Gary Lineker's jumper choices, some tears and laughter about nostalgic TV programmes, finishing up with a sense that maybe you should pop in on your Grandad more because what's life all about at the end of the day. And all of that was under an hour. We didn't seek an outcome.

Something started to appear in the human experience in 1914. Soldiers in the British Expeditionary Force were exhibiting strange symptoms. They were losing the ability to speak, sudden unexplained blindness, memory loss, hysteria, paralysis and suicidal thoughts. By 1916, 40% of all British casualties in the First World War were due to this condition. In 1917 a medical officer called Charles Myers coined the phrase: Shell Shock. Some 80,000 cases had passed through medical services by the end of the war, 16,000 of them coming from the Battle of the Somme alone. By the end of the war, 20 hospitals were set up to deal with it.

At first the medical profession thought it was a physiological problem, although some believe this view was taken because those working in psychiatry were keen to be taken more seriously by the rest of the medical profession. Treatments were brutal – putting soldiers in solitary confinement, shouting commands at them day and night, giving them electric shocks and starving them. It all sort of reminds me of a "course of leeches" doled out by quacks centuries before. However, different approaches emerged at this time and in many ways provided the basis for what would become modern psychiatry.

Dr Arthur Hirst in Seale Hayne hospital in Devon used a form of Occupational Therapy. The soldiers would work in the fields and help run the farm. This purposeful activity had excellent results. Hirst claimed to "cure" 90% of cases. The most famous of the modern approaches though was in Craiglockhart in Scotland. You may know it from the brilliant Pat Barker *Regeneration* trilogy or the feature film by Gillies Mackinnon. Here an army doctor called W. H. Rivers developed a "talking cure". He would educate the soldiers in psychology and then revisit their terrible experiences of the war in order to unearth repressed feelings and ultimately rob the experiences of their power. It's hard to believe that this was revolutionary but it wasn't just going against the prevailing winds of medical opinion, it was also the time of "stiff upper lip", so men didn't talk about these things let alone cry about them.

Rivers also made an important discovery that influenced how armed forces the world over trained their troops thereafter. He discovered that the way soldiers continued to fight and overcome their paralysing fear was not, as the press and the Government would have us believe, King and Country, glory or wanting to kill the enemy, but was in fact the soldiers' love for one another. They stuck with their buddy to the left or the right of them. This was the prime motivation. There are few times in human history when we have been closer to annihilation and Armageddon than the First World War, and the trenches were among the very worst of times. Yet I find it hopeful, if that isn't inappropriate, that the only thing that got these young men through this hell was looking out for each other. If that's what it takes to get through "Armageddon" maybe it'll work for us getting through our own tough times and tricky days!

However my main fascination with this historical event for the purposes of this chapter is not about Rivers and Hirst's use of Friends and Purpose but more about what the rest of the establishment did. The predominant approach was to "fix" the problem as if it were physical, much like a mechanic would reach for a spanner to fix an engine. The electric shock treatment leaves us horrified, yet are we so different today? It is only recently that people have acknowledged that mental health should have the same attention as physical and this is almost a century later – and we're still not there yet. I would also suggest that this electric shock approach to fixing is prevalent in anytime we try to systemise a solution – we do not think of Rivers and pursue the human, talking approach when a sign, an angry notice, a harshly designed environment would, in our opinion, engineer the right results and make people bend to our will.

Much like the psychiatrists back then, we find it hard to be taken seriously by proposing Friends and Purpose as the solution to society's problems. People do not want to hear that drug addiction can be solved by human connection[3]. They want a Taskforce and hard-hitting interventions. When they look at the root causes of homelessness or criminal activity they want to find something they can stamp out. Every now and again there will be a mission statement or a campaign about "Ending ...." (insert societal problem here). They don't want to hear that there will always be pain and suffering and people will dip in and out of it their whole life, probably. This being the case we could resist the tough language of "ending" thus raising unrealistic expectations – and perhaps a bit of stigma too. Hard-hitting targets tend to inspire hard-hitting strategies and that almost never includes the fundamental need to build relationships. Relationships are gentle things that take time. People "ending" social problems don't want hugging and talking, thanks very much! If the minister is to make a speech about it, he wants numbers, data, magic wand solutions. Never mind that once that new moment passes, the people inside the data just end up falling apart again and nothing changes over time.

This need to fix is, of course, in all of us. I'm the worst at this. My wife always says that I started a social movement based on everything I'm crap at. I underperform on all the Camerados principles. And the worst is the fixing one. Just being alongside people, not diving in with an answer, I find it hard. I also discovered that often better things happen when I leave the room. Sometimes I take up way too much oxygen and need to leave

3   Hari, Johann, *Chasing the Scream : the First and Last Days of the War on Drugs*. New York: Bloomsbury, 2015.

so others can speak. As someone who derives a major part of their own personal validation from taking responsibility and being involved, this is excruciatingly hard for me at times.

Just because we don't set out to fix things doesn't mean nothing is achieved!

I think there is some kind of separation going on here between the intent when we are doing something, and how that drives our behaviour and what happens as a result. We don't seek an outcome, and by doing the "not seeking" a better outcome is achieved. Seeking out that outcome so pointedly and explicitly seems to spoil its chances of organically appearing.

Once, one man came up to me after an event where I was speaking in a state of great restlessness. "I think I'm a fixer, I didn't realise I've been doing it wrong all these years." He talked to me about how he often offers up ideas and advice to people in the community project where he works. He ran a "befriending service" and his advice was always well meant, he said. Was he making a horrible mistake all this time?

I asked him to give himself a break. In the course of normal conversation we all offer up thoughts, but there's a difference in saying "You know what something worked for me? I go to this place on a Wednesday etc.", and a fixer saying "Right what you have to do is go to this place on a Wednesday. It's at two o'clock. I've made the appointment, you're going, I'll check to see you've gone!". One is just a conversation where the person listening doesn't have to follow your advice, while the other sounds like an instruction and is definitely "fixing". Thankfully the man looked seriously relieved, though I obviously reminded him I'm not the arbiter of what he should or shouldn't do, it's just what we've learnt works.

We've found over the years that we've been doing this public living room approach – maybe some people in coats with pens might call it a "social experiment" – that so many people get a huge amount of solace and comfort from being in a position where they are not expected to do anything. Where nobody is "in their face" with a solution to their problems. Like Alan in Hastings sitting in Wetherspoons, not being bothered by anyone. Except Alan was alone. In public living rooms people could do this with others. It can be liberating to set out to achieve nothing in the company of others.

Taking the pressure off from finding an answer seems to do many things. It seems to equalise a relationship between people, if you're not trying to fix me, not coming with any agenda, then we can just share experiences without having to go anywhere in particular. We can just be fellow travellers rather than doctor and patient. It also allows for creativity to blossom. Unconstrained from one person's desired outcome to another's problems, the mind opens to ideas as yet un-entertained. Why not consider the previously unconsidered if nobody is checking on progress? There doesn't need to be progress, we're just talking.

There was an expression on people's faces I used to dread. Over twenty years of working in institutions and very traditional services for people with all sorts of "issues" I would always try to build a rapport first. I'd talk about nothing in particular, just be alongside them. However, eventually I'd start leading the conversation towards their "support plan" and the issue I had to resolve with them as my "client". This was the point the person would realise that this perfectly lovely conversation they were having was not one between equals, not the one they were enjoying with someone who was interested in them only as a fellow human connecting with them, but in fact this was a professional relationship between key worker and service user. It was a transaction. The expression that came over their face when they realised this was one of disappointment. It is the expression made when humanity walks out the door. That's how it felt to me. I've been trying to avoid it ever since. I've noticed that if my body language, my topics of conversation, my chosen words seem to say, "I am here just cos we're talking, I'm interested in you just because, and this doesn't have to go anywhere" then things always seem to flourish and go better after that. We actually get to the support plan issues anyway most of the time, and if we don't then we've still had a connection and a good conversation which is hugely beneficial.

Aiming to achieve nothing takes effort!

I need to warn you though. I called this chapter a "revolution" because this "no solution" business takes some effort. You are swimming against a tide. What you will be doing is not popular and people just cannot get their head around it. This may be the challenge we've witnessed more than any other in the ten years we've been doing this Camerados thing. For something so deliberately light touch it's a bit depressing how fiercely you have to protect a public living room.

Such are the levels you have to go to just to keep it free of "projects", free of agenda, free of "success" that the whole area of nothingness takes on something of an other worldly vibe – it doesn't belong in our noisy, solution driven society. We have seen people feel the need to fill it with smoking cessation classes; public consultations on council strategy; surgeries for the local ward councillors. Daisy in the Rochdale public living room (a beautiful little space in a community centre fashioned from donated clocks and sofas which looks just like your Granny's living room) has to physically bar the path of local politicians from walking in. She stretches her arms across the door frame and screams, laughing, "You can't do that here!".

My favourite example is Tameside hospital in Manchester where they filled it with white rabbits. Yep, opening day of the hospital public living room and everywhere you looked, white, lolloping bunnies. It turned out the space had been colonised by a visiting pet therapy group. What's the problem with lovely cuddly bunny rabbits you say? Well, not everyone wants to get away from it all only to find 20 or 30 big-toothed lagomorphs (I googled it). The space isn't about emotional wellbeing animals or therapy of any sort; even if that's a lovely thing it might not be *everyone's* thing.

As I'm writing this today, an email has arrived from a friend who I *hugely* respect from the world of community action, who runs one of the biggest public living rooms around and is more informed than most, and yet they are asking if we can get funding from a Climate Change fund for public living rooms. It seems they think it would be a great space to "introduce a climate perspective to a group". You see this is where it gets mighty difficult. This is where it upsets people. It's a fantastic thing to educate people about climate change, of course it is, but what if a climate change denier wants to come in? They've had a hard day and need a bit of company, and they just happen to think fossil fuels are fine. And then someone "introduces a climate perspective to them", and I'm guessing they'd leave. Truth is they wouldn't come through the door in the first place. The agenda would exclude them.

Making sure there's one place that everyone can go where there is no agenda, nobody in your face, no need to succeed at anything … . turns out to be way harder than you'd imagine.

So I invite you to join the No Solution Revolution. Go against the grain of society and stop looking for the outcome. Stop being so constantly aware of the success story you can put on your socials later. Put the kettle on and talk bollocks. It's a much more profound thing than I think most of us realise.

Public living rooms
from around the world

Hastings

HARTLEPOOL

Dawn sat down and let out a long gasp. She was maybe in her forties, white blouse and skirt and a sensible beige jacket. "Am I too heavy for this thing?" she said, lowering herself onto the sofa. I honestly didn't know what to say without fear of conveying some opinion about Dawn's weight. Thankfully, local camerado Esme was sitting with us and told her to put her arse down on the sofa and if it collapsed we'd have a right good laugh anyway! Dawn screeched with laughter and plonked herself down, without damage to herself or furniture. Esme never seems to have a problem being brilliantly honest with folk, verging on the rude, whilst never making them feel she's anything other than on their side. A rare talent. Or maybe everyone in the North East has it.

When I met Esme she looked like I imagine Uriah Heap from Dickens' *David Copperfield* to look. Sullen, unhappy, dowdy dresser, never smiled, but whenever she spoke she had phenomenally great ideas, which we encouraged her to share because then we could steal them and pass them off as our own. Unfortunately she stayed very engaged with the movement and our work so we could never quite get away with the last bit without her noticing. She is fiercely bright, talks very quickly and precisely and is never short of completely honest. She lives with the kind of chronic illness that saps you of all energy and on some days means you can't get down the stairs.

She has a man that lives in her head called Horace who tells her awful things about herself daily, mostly that everything around her is terrifying. When the pandemic hit, things got better, surprisingly. Suddenly she wasn't the only one not going out of the house, somehow this helped, she wasn't the one missing out all the time or being construed as weak or lazy anymore. Horace disappeared for a while. It was bliss.

Sadly Horace is back now but she's onto his wily ways and with the help of her irrepressibly positive and gag-cracking husband and genius-level kids she is doing great. Despite all these difficulties Esme will often appear in my WhatsApp messages asking me about my black dogs and letting me ask her about Horace. Neither of us have any answers for each other – it doesn't work like that. I'm just crazy proud that she wants to know me to be honest.

Today in Hartlepool she sports a wildly fashionable punk hairstyle half black, half white, a fabulous red coat, pointy shoes and has turned Uriah Heap into a sort of steampunk/8os pop kick ass heroine. Why did I tell you all that? I just want you to know about brilliant people who turn things around in the face of adversity and yet aren't Presidents, Olympic sportsmen or TV celebrities on the front of your newspaper. Heroic legends exist on your street. In Hartlepool.

Esme and Dawn had something in common and after talk of the Tall Ships race – coming to Hartlepool later that year – subsided, they discovered it. "I've not left the house for the best part of five years," Dawn said. She had been redundant and it had happened totally out of the blue. She wondered now if she'd had her head in the clouds – she's gone over it so many times. The way they told her was awful; she had to leave by a side entrance with a box of all her stuff and she couldn't say goodbye to anyone. It totally knocked her confidence. She couldn't get a job after that which just made things worse. "I couldn't go out, what if I saw someone," she said, and she told me and Esme a familiar story about the phases of growing chronic isolation. Her health suffered, she said. We sat with her while she said nothing for a while. Cars whizzed past. Neither Esme or I wanted to interrupt her thoughts, which were busy and filling the silent air.

"But things are looking up," she said. "I just did half an hour in the pub yesterday." She told us that she'd done really well, talked to the barman and a few of the customers, about nothing really but it was nice. The only thing is that she's really kicking herself because as she walked out she slipped on the step and nearly fell flat on the floor on the pavement outside the pub. "I bet they all saw that. I haven't been able to stop thinking about it, it's daft isn't it but I couldn't sleep."

Jeremy wore grey slacks, driving gloves hanging out the rear pocket, a natty flat cap, cheeky smile and bounded up so confidently I thought he was going to sell me a caravan. "I'm an identical twin," he said. Not a common conversation opener I grant you but it got interesting pretty quickly. "We have the same thoughts you know!" I was doubting the validity of Jeremy's assertion and told him he'd watched too many episodes of *The Twilight Zone* or that other TV programme that had the sexy titles from the 1970s, *"Tales of the Unexpected"* Esme informed us. "It's true," Jeremy continued. "Me and my brother bought the exact same car, same colour. And we bought the exact same caravan." I knew he'd have a caravan. "Well to be fair," continued Jeremy, "his was a six berth but it was close."

WORDS WE DON'T USE ENOUGH

I don't know.

What do you think?

WORDS WE USE TOO OFTEN

What you should do is ...

I'm gonna fix this.

CARDIFF

PART TWO

Cardiff has managed to block off all entry to vehicles to the centre of town. Every turn I make in town I come across a steel bollard blocking my path. Fantastic for the planet, a right bugger for a street activist with a van. I park miles away and carry the furniture in several trips until I make it outside the main library and opposite John Lewis. By the time I sit down I'm breaking a serious sweat.

A woman looks at me. "I know you," she says. She tells me that she'd heard me speak a couple of years ago and follows me on social media. She saw I was in town today and, as she happened to be out having lunch for her birthday with her mum, she thought she'd seek me out. Her mum was in her eighties and a wise owl with a cunning smile behind thick-rimmed glasses. I can tell she found it kind of mystifying that this was how people meet nowadays. The three of us sat opposite the public living room (sometimes it's good just to leave it to populate itself) and we started to chat about why my talk had interested her and then about the ripples of influence that our actions can make and at this point her mother told us she had her own remarkable instance of this. A young man had come up to her about ten or fifteen years ago and said that he had been a student in her economics class at university. He said that her ideas had changed the course of his life. After taking her class, he decided to become an economist and focus on a particular area and excel at it. He was now advising President Barack Obama in the White House. I was open mouthed; the old lady smiled and her daughter laughed. "Yeah my mum is kind of ace," she said. We talked some more and then this five foot tall elderly lady, slightly bent over, wearing a comfy cardigan and out for lunch with her daughter, waved me goodbye and wandered off to no doubt inspire and influence some more minds, nations, Presidents.

The second remarkable story of the day came via a punnet of plums. They suddenly appeared on a mobility scooter offered up by a rotund fella with a kind smile who glided up to us on his slightly knackered little transport and held out a plastic tub from the local market. He offered them around the group of strangers in the public living room, each of whom took them readily and with a laugh and immediately struck up a conversation with him. This was Daniel and he was a softly spoken guy who, upon hearing what we were doing and what Camerados was all about, opened up to my colleague about his story. He spoke about it as if revealing a secret golden egg he kept hidden on his person at all times. It was his special possession; his story made him feel rich – it was the thing that always stopped people in their tracks, he knew it would, and it did.

It happened when he was a teenager. He was from up North, Yorkshire way, and had run away from home. He didn't say why he'd run away but just that he got as far as a service station on the M1 where he sat down and drew a sign that read, "Anywhere but here".

A long-distance lorry driver called Trevor walked past, saw the sign and offered him breakfast. Over a fried feast, Trevor asked him about the sign, they chatted a bit and then he offered him a lift in his truck. He was going as far as Cardiff and then was heading off into Europe but could take him as far as the Welsh capital. Daniel accepted the lift and travelled south with Trevor.

Later that day they pulled over so Trevor could sleep but he gave the young runaway his bunk while he kipped in the driving seat. They talked for hours as they drove through the rain and wind towards Wales. Daniel said the conversation was easy, like it is with strangers. He commented that it wasn't until they got to Leigh Delamere services for a toilet stop and a coffee that he found out Trevor's name, yet for hours he'd told him all his secrets and all his woes. When they got to the centre of Cardiff, Trevor told him to wait by the lorry while he made a phone call and ran a quick errand. He thought this a bit weird but didn't say anything. On returning to the truck Trevor handed him his luggage, gave him a firm handshake and wished him well. As he drove off Daniel opened his bag to find a thousand pounds inside. Beside the money was Trevor's phone number and a note saying to give him a call if he wanted to meet up for a chat and a coffee. At this point in the story our narrator took a moment to compose himself. He told us what that had meant to him, a stranger doing this for him.

He'd used the money to get a place to live and set himself up in Cardiff. In the time that followed he got himself a decent job and had done well for himself, but his big regret was that, though he'd kept Trevor's bag, somehow the note with the phone number was gone. It haunted him that he couldn't find it; he'd looked everywhere, turned his digs upside down several times. Years passed and now with a wife and kids he was having a sort-out in his house before a camping trip, when he came across Trevor's bag again. He gave it one last look for the number and remarkably there it was, hidden all this time inside the lining of the bag by the zip. He leapt up and ran down the stairs to the phone. A woman answered and on hearing who it was, said: "I wondered if you'd ever call love." It was Trevor's wife. She told him that she remembered that night very clearly. Daniel remembered when Trevor dropped him off in Cardiff saying he had to make a call and run an errand; well, the call was to his wife it seemed. She said he had explained that he'd met this lad on the side of the road and that he wanted to give him a thousand pounds. That was a lot of money, not money they could afford back then, but she heard in his voice that he felt it was the right thing to do and she gave her blessing. The errand he ran was to get the money out of the bank. Daniel told her he just wanted to thank him personally and would she mind putting him on the phone. There was a little silence on the other end of the phone. "I'm sorry love," she said, "but he passed away a couple of months ago."

It's fair to say that everyone in the pavement public living room was spellbound, sat in silence, wide eyed but saying nothing, forming tears. Daniel never got to thank Trevor and tell him what his kindness had meant to his life. To the sound of sniffs and wiping of eyes, our narrator told us that he was still in touch with Trevor's wife. They had become friends and had even held a few small fundraising events for things Trevor cared about.

We all just sat silently and took in what we had heard.

Then the mood changed and we all marveled at the story and paid tribute to Trevor. Daniel seemed really happy at the reaction of all these strangers. We stayed and chatted for a while, bonded by the experience, the day we heard that remarkable story.

71

BAD KINDNESS

The idea that kindness can be bad

Having worked in and around charities for 30 years I've come to the conclusion it's not enough to be kind. It's *how* we are kind that matters.

Aren't we told that to be kind is the most important thing? Didn't Tom Hanks say that? You don't want to contradict Tom Hanks. Or THanks as I've just decided to call him. No, that doesn't really work.

As a matter of fact, every single morning for as long as my kids have been going to school, the last thing I say to them as they head out the door is "Be Kind and be interested". So then, why is kindness not enough?

That's because kindness is done badly a lot of the time and absolutely nobody talks about it. Lots of people do really kind things and it's one of the big taboos to criticise them. It's like punching a puppy. So welcome folks to the puppy punching chapter!

In 1993 I went along to volunteer at some homeless shelters with a halo over my head. All my friends told me what a helluva good guy I was for giving up my Christmas week to spend it in a place for "down and out" drinkers and even more impressive I was working the night shift from 10pm until 8am in the morning. I glowed with inner goodness. So it was a bit of a shock then when I met these folk in the homeless shelter and discovered that they, in fact, got *me* through that Christmas, not the other way around.

Being connected requires us to know a little about each other; I'm gonna stop here and let you have a bit of personal context. I ought to tell you that the most profound connection I have had to people in my life started with my Mum and Dad. I was blessed with brilliant, funny, loving siblings but they all left home when I was ten years old because they were quite a bit older than me, so for all of my teens I was a bit like an only child. That was no hardship whatsoever because, unlike some people, I got on great with my folks. Dad was my hero and best friend, He was a complete original. If I ever go back to my hometown of Carlisle I swear someone asks me if I'm "Mick Potts's son" at least 3 times a day. He either employed them in his textile mill (until it went bust in the recession and we lost everything) or much more likely entertained them with his Jazz band or through his radio or TV show. He was larger than life, hugely gregarious, helped everyone out and had a massive enquiring mind. I was a weird kid, I'd cancel going out with friends because I wanted to stay in and hang out with Dad. My mum was our north star and the boss of the family. Quiet, kept her own counsel, opposite of Dad in that she was a very private person with a private faith. We found out much later she'd been helping out families in our community without our knowledge. She was in some ways fearsome too and if we didn't roll up our sleeves and get the work done around the house we knew about it. Yet her love and fun was infectious and I can only dance because she would grab me as I walked through the kitchen and jive and jitterbug with me while the radio was on. The three of us would travel and holiday together, and go for walks, walks where I remember they always held hands.

Sorry if that sounds sentimental but what can I say, I was a very lucky kid. I'm telling you about it because that Christmas when I volunteered for the homeless shelters was the same year that Dad died from a heart attack, three days before my 21st birthday. They say he died of a broken heart because Mum had already died three years earlier from breast cancer, same week of the year, three days after my 18th birthday. And to this day people are still mystified why I don't celebrate my birthday. As wonderful as those siblings were, they already had children of their own and probably out of some daft pride I wanted to do my own thing that first Christmas without Mum and Dad so I went to the shelters instead of going to their houses, despite their invitations.

As I say, because it bears repeating, I discovered that these people with nothing, who were homeless, they got *me* through that Christmas, not the other way around. I found that people with far greater problems than me – and so much less in life – made me a cup of tea and beat me at Scrabble. They'd take me into their confidence and treat me like an equal. Despite having lived many more lives than I could own up to as a young, wet-behind-the-ears, middle-class white boy, none of the homeless guests in that shelter ever talked down to me. My much-missed Dad never did that either – he was quite remarkable in that respect – and as such the equality and mutuality that these people bestowed on our interactions that first Christmas without him was more appreciated that I can put into words. It ingrained in me a deep belief in that kind of mutual respect and gave me kinship for people who have absolutely bugger all, and who society just can't resist talking to in a funny, patronising voice full of jargon and nonsense.

We were all there together under the stars of a Christmas night, drinking out of polystyrene cups and passing round the Rothmans Superkings so naturally it would have been very embarrassing to set myself up as the one who was there to "help" them. That would have put a distance between us when it felt like we were all in the shit together.

That parent–child dynamic that charity places on situations is "bad kind-ness". Which is why dressing up kindness in rainbows and love hearts – as people so often do – just adds to the infantilising vibe. The person receiv-ing kindness is somehow patted on the head by the fairy-tale do-gooder. The arrogance and selfishness is pretty bad.

I don't think it's a problem at all for people to do kind acts because it makes them feel good, I think that's entirely right and I wish people were more open and honest about it. We all like to see ourselves as a little bit of a hero. The problems arrive when it guides some of our behaviours, it often leads you to play a role that insists others play their role too. If you are a "hero" then it's important that the people you "rescue" are feckless. Also they need to be grateful. So therefore you just can't help talk down to them, just ever-so slightly. You just can't help but expect less of them too. And, of course, as a hero you assume they will accept whatever charity you give them, cos you know what's best for them, right? Being a hero and all!

But at least these people are doing good, I hear you say as you shield the "puppy" from me.

Well not really. Is it doing good to make someone feel rubbish about themselves? To lose some of their dignity? When you are at an all-time low in life, the behaviour of others towards you can seriously tip you over the edge, stripping you of the last dregs of confidence you had left.

It's worse than just the parent–child dynamic; it's a parent who makes it all about *them*. Think about some kind interactions we may have all had:

• Did you think about the language you use when you deliver kindness in order to make the person feel less "helped"?

• Did you properly check whether or not the person actually wanted the gift or the kind act? Did you ask them?

• Was it unimportant to you whether they thanked you properly?

• Was it unimportant to you somehow that people knew that you had done a kind act?

• Did you build any kind of rapport with them, find out about their life, was there a relationship alongside whatever gift you gave?

That last one, the relationship bit, is probably the most crucial cos it tends to take care of the rest. If you see the person as a human I believe the chances are most people will treat that person with equality and dignity. Perhaps I've misunderstood kindness but I think the absence of the above considerations can lead to the other person feeling less good about themselves and to me that's not being kind.

People ask me all the time "Should I give to beggars?". I always say that I don't know because I don't know the person they are talking about. Beggars aren't one homogenous mass of like-minded individuals. Isn't it better to ask yourself if you looked the 'beggar' in the eye, said hello and asked their name first? I find it funny that the financial transaction is always the first thought – should I give them money? How many other social situations do we go into where this is our first concern? At a party do you walk up to people you've never met before and say, "I can't give you any money." Why should meeting this "beggar" on the street be any different? They are a person and you don't know them, so get to know them before you talk money, no?

One of the reasons the "no fixing principle" is useful in this context is that if you liberate yourself from the notion that it is beholden upon you to solve a beggar's entire life problems then maybe you'd relax and behave like a human. So if you don't have time to stop then just say so and do it with a smile; if you do have time then get to know them. Then you can make an informed choice about this money transaction too. What that person does with your money, with your kindness, well that's not up to you anymore ... you got to know them a little and you gave the money to them. You might decide you think they will use it on drugs and you may think that this will harm them more and you may not like that, so then don't give them the money. You may think the opposite, however. This will only come from a chat.

Chances are that every freedom has been taken away from someone begging in the street, so perhaps once we've got to know them a little we can leave the choice to spend the money on what they like, up to them. Trevor (from the previous chapter) spent a long journey getting to know Daniel, and this helped him decide that he wanted to make a pretty life-changing donation to him. It meant something to Daniel because he too knew something about Trevor; they had a connection. It was Trevor's trust in Daniel that meant something not just the money; he had faith in him.

Would it have meant the same if Trevor had dumped some cash on Daniel that first time he saw him and just kept on walking? I don't think so. I wonder how Daniel would have spent the cash if that had been the transaction. Sure, you could say that Trevor was trying to fix Daniel with the cash, but listening to the story it didn't feel like that. He was just alongside him and at that point in time he had the means to help a bit. The phone number, the connection was as important to Daniel.

As with all these ideas, none of them are new or radical and either the Quakers (I'm a lifelong fan) or Charles Dickens came up with most of them 150 years before me. In the Quakers' case, make that 350 years before! As for Dickens he wrote in *Bleak House*:

"There were two classes of charitable people: one, the people who did a little and made a great deal of noise; the other, the people who did a great deal and made no noise at all."

In the book, Mrs Pardiggle practically forces down the doors of "the poor" in order to read the Bible at them for their own improvement. Dickens writes:

"Mrs Pardiggle being as clear that the only one infallible course was her course of pouncing upon the poor, and applying benevolence to them like a strait-waistcoat."

On the one hand you have Scrooge in "A Christmas Carol" reviling the poor and preferring they would die and here you have the Victorian philanthropists viewing them as no less a commodity.

(I will talk about Scrooge and Dickens in a later chapter because having worked in those streets in London's East end that he so brilliantly brought to life I can say that few writers – Orwell being another – have had the personal experience and empathy to truly capture how it feels to live there. Ignore your school prejudices, Dickens is the man!)

So now that I've shot your puppy you really don't wanna read on, right?! I get it. I'd rather you did, though; also that you got in touch and put me right. In Camerados we believe very strongly in disagreeing well. So send me an email to maff@Camerados.org and set me straight. I'd love it! Better still, let's have a cuppa.

LIVERPOOL

If you seek honest feedback go to Liverpool.

"Are you taking the fuckin' piss mate?"

I'd barely got the furniture out of the van. The fella who was shouting in my ear was living on the streets and there was I unloading a sofa, some armchairs, a rug and some houseplants and putting them on the cobbles just beside his spot. I could see his point.

The next day in Toxteth, an area south of the city centre, a woman was sat on the front step outside her house in a row of red terraces wearing a onesie covered in watermelons and pandas and jabbing her cigarette at me, saying:

"I asked you a fuckin' question nob-end."

I explained what we were doing. "Well ya fucking public living shite is gonna attract all the scum we've only just cleared out of that fuckin place," she gestured towards the grassy bit of wasteland at the end of the terraced houses where we'd put our pop up public living room. "We've only just cleaned the place up and now you're gonna bring all the greasy f*ckers back."

I didn't want to get into it so just apologised, acknowledged it was her street not mine and that we'd be out of her hair soon enough. At this her friend – two doors down, also sat on her step, also smoking, also wearing a onesie (she'd gone for unicorns and rainbows) – interrupted her friend and said, "Not to worry pet, it's a nice thing you're doing."

Angela wasn't convinced. "F*cking public living shite." I did feel like a do-gooding, middle class "nob-end" parachuting into someone else's neighbourhood that day thinking I had something to offer.

Not that our Liverpool trip was all like this. Far from it. In the city centre we had a succession of human stories sitting down with us and resting a while as the rest of the city bustled passed, it seemed like hundreds every minute. There was the shy engineering student from Peru who lingered on the edges of us for half an hour before finally entering the conversation with an observation about Newton's third law of thermodynamics. He sat beside me confounding the shy stereotype I'd constructed for him by sharing with me his dream to be an inventor who changed the course of history. He was pretty convinced his sustainable, eco-friendly ocean-going super tankers would be a game changer. I kept my observation about the very unsustainable oil inside the super tankers to myself.

Then there was the young, intense-looking man who worked in an office nearby and felt compelled to tell me his very strong connection with "this Camerados thing". He didn't find it easy being with people but didn't want to be alone either – just being around people would be good. He had a breakdown earlier that year and knew locking himself away hadn't helped. He told me that although he didn't like his work he had stayed in the company for four years because he really liked the people in the office.

Then there were the three very charismatic, chatty, hilarious girls from a local college who slumped down on the sofas and proceeded to tell us stories about their dysfunctional teachers. They were undecided about whether to exact revenge on the frumpy one who was particularly horrible to them in class as they had found out, with a bit of expert googling, that Ms Frumpy was selling sex toys on-line and seemed to have a fetish for her boyfriend's feet. They showed us the pictures on their phone and I might have had some moral quibbles had they not had us all in stitches.

Yet again, as in Belfast, stood opposite us all day were evangelical preachers doing their "repent or burn" thing loudly through a mic and speaker outside Primark. A visitor, a well spoken MAMIL (middle aged man in Lycra), wearing those cyclists sunglasses that look like ski goggles, had been pouring over the messages on our coasters and the little concertina leaflets we have that talk about the Camerados movement. He said he was enjoying the juxtaposition. I asked him what he meant. "You couldn't get a more stark difference between you lot and the God Squad over there," he said. "I'm a Christian myself so it's not the religion I object to but the methods of public engagement are worth remarking upon." "Methods?" I say. "Yeah, this fella is literally yelling at people telling them we're all God's people and telling them to mend their ways, fix their sins and they'll achieve eternal life. Here you are with a bunch of disparate strangers sat on a sofa not not mending or minding each other's ways in the least and not much caring if you're going to hell as long as you have some company on the way." I could've kissed him. "You've got it mate."

Back in Toxteth we had just had a lovely chat with a local community worker who told us the area was newly populated by mostly Romani families when a swaggering presence appeared among us. A Romani man with a baseball gap, baggy pants and a bit of bling around his neck appeared with an entourage of teenage boys. They invaded our space with a deliberate air of ownership and the kingpin character immediately made me an offer for our furniture. I told him we weren't selling but he was persistent. It transpired that he was moving into a new house that day and had no furniture. His wife and five kids had been living with a friend but now they'd finally got their own place. He showed me some "before" pictures of the new house on his phone and there was room after room of knee deep rubbish and broken fences outside the house. Then he swiped left and showed me his handiwork from the last week – clean painted walls, empty clean rooms and patched up fencing.

I broke a big Camerado principle – the one that says our spaces are not for fixing problems but just being alongside. I said he could have two of our chairs. I suppose I couldn't stand being the middle-class idiot with my lovely stuff anymore and just caved to someone whose need was greater than ours. It seemed right, in the moment, but of course the point of what we were doing on the streets was to sell the idea of human connection not give away furniture. Old notions of Victorian charity live deep inside all of us just waiting for guilt to awaken it. However, I got a chance to slightly redeem myself, when he gave me the chance to bring out another Camerados principle to good effect with him later.

We arranged a time for me to drop them around his house but the conversations of the day had overtaken us and we stayed chatting to strangers long after the time that I had said we'd be there. He turned up in his friend's car and was not happy. As we loaded the van he started to demand more furniture from me. He used every guilt-inducing tactic in the book until eventually he just went for straight begging and would not accept my refusals. In the end I carried the two chairs to his car and asked his friend to take them. His friend was lovely and happily put them in his car boot. I turned to my swaggering friend and told him not to piss people off who were doing him favours and giving him very nice chairs. I told him that he made people feel bad who were being kind and that he should give me a little more respect. His children were here and they don't need to see their dad treat someone like this. He shuffled in his baggy trousers a bit and moved his baseball cap to a more rogue-ish, cool angle. He had nothing to say. I asked him if we understood each other and he nodded. I smiled, shook his hand and bid him farewell.

Feeling rather pleased with myself, thinking that I'd done the Camerado thing of being straight with him and "disagreeing respectfully" to restore some semblance of mutuality rather than charity I was – again – brought back down to earth with a jolt and a sense of my own failure when I returned to the van and found several Romani families – about 25 people – surrounding it, hoping to get their free chairs too. This is where charity gets you.

Back in the city centre our sofas and armchairs were in the paved pedestrianised street outside the shop and gaming café known as Geek Retreat. The lovely folk there were in the movement too and held a pop-up public living room in the store now and again. Out of the shop carrying a Geek Retreat bag wandered a small round man in a denim jacket and trousers and a woman in cobalt blue dungarees. Chace and his girlfriend are hairdressers and when they sat down on my sofa they just watched the world go by and fell into the kind of comfortable silence long-term couples do so well.

"I run an inclusive salon," says Chase, "because many trans and gay customers have been bullied by other salons when they ask for what they want." He told me of this magical place he has created, full of colour, music, hot tea and hair styles both lavish and everyday. A place of conversations about nail colours and yesterday's vicious abuse all mingled in with the sound of scissors clattering and chopping. Apparently the shop was small and on the corner of an unremarkable street but by the time Chace had stopped telling me about it truly felt like the most marvellous and important place in the world.

I'm not proud to say I felt fear when the teenagers approached. A whole crowd of them, mostly boys but a couple of girls, dressed in black tops with the hoods up swooped in, it happened in seconds. They colonised the public living room immediately. I expected trouble and couldn't imagine anyone else would want to sit down as long as they were there. I couldn't have been more wrong. As time passed they casually invited passersby to take a seat, take them on at Connect Four, or just have conversation whilst passing. One young lad on the sofa next to me taught me some sign language. It turned out his mate was deaf so they'd all learnt it so he could still feel part of the gang. I thought this must be bravado but his deaf mate actually turned up later on and I saw all of them sign to him at some point.

Another lad told me a bit about his life. He'd been kipping in doorways in the city centre until one day the others had stopped to talk to him. Apparently, even though he was looking pretty grubby living on the streets, they could make out that his baseball cap was by a niche American designer that the rest of the gang all really liked. In fact they all wore the same stuff. It transpired that all of them were celebrity autograph hunters. They would hear on social media that a cast member of Hollyoaks was at a bar in the town and, like volunteer fireman getting the signal, would call each other and run for buses into town so that they could wait outside the bar. They recruited the homeless lad into their number and put him up on their sofa. "I swear to God this lot are my family now. I didn't get on too well with my own, dad was violent, so I lived with all this lot until I got my own place."

I took a phone call, it was BBC Liverpool saying they were coming down to interview me so I asked the journalist if he wouldn't mind interviewing the young hoodie crew instead and he agreed. This brush with media and celebrity status was like winning the jackpot it seemed. They couldn't contain their excitement and chatted to the guy with his big furry microphone for ages; they wouldn't let him go. Afterwards they kept grabbing their own heads and saying, "That was wild, man". Later on I felt sad when I had to break up the party and went to get the van. As I opened the back doors the young formerly homeless lad said, "Maff, leave this to us." One by one they dismantled the public living room for me and carried all the furniture into the van. I didn't lift a finger. Then as I closed the doors and turned round to thank them, they were stood facing me and their de facto leader, a ginger-haired lad with a permanent grin, handed me a box of Roses chocolates. "We clubbed together and wanted to get you these to say thanks, we've had a mega day."

Youth of today eh?!

THE 6 MOST POWERFUL WORDS IN THE ENGLISH LANGUAGE

*The idea that when people are in trouble
maybe sometimes we don't help them
but do something else instead*

The guy on the end of the phone was an ambulance driver and he asked me if I ran a Mexican restaurant. I told him that "Camerados" was actually a social movement trying to find a better, more human way through tough times, but I did like the occasional burrito and he wasn't the first person to ask. He said there was a woman in his ambulance who was saying that she wanted to go to the pier and throw herself into the sea. He'd heard about our place and wondered if he could drop her off with us instead.

When the woman arrived she seemed surprised by the bunting and fairy lights, the plants and the linen tablecloths and the fella playing "Sweet Caroline" really badly on the piano. She threaded her way through the sofas and armchairs dotted around our corner of Blackpool's grand, red-bricked public library. I could see by her confused expression that the people around her were such an odd mix of folk – old, young, posh, poor, ordinary, strange – that she wasn't getting any clues about what this place was supposed to be. I found out that her name was Beverley and she didn't take sugar in her tea. She was short with a blonde bob, a nose ring, thick green eye shadow and on top of her jeans she wore a pink heavy sweatshirt with blood splattered down it from her left eye where her husband had, that afternoon, pushed her down the stairs. She looked broken and couldn't look me in the eye when I offered her two mugs of hot tea. I said I was sorry she was having such a rough day and asked her if she could do me a favour and take the other mug to Colin, an old man sat on his mobility scooter at the corner table wearing an army beret and camouflage jacket. Colin was having a particularly lonely day and I told her it would be great if she could have a cuppa with him and lift his spirits. She obliged.

Colin was a regular. The people up at the hospital called him a "High Intensity User" because he used to ring 999 about twenty times a day. He does this primarily to talk to somebody and there are a lot more people who do this on a daily basis than you might realise. He was chronically lonely but not long after he started coming to our place he began to buy little plants and put them on the tables and water them each day. Nobody had asked him to do that, but somehow he just knew he could if he wanted to, so he did, and when we all thanked him and told him it was brilliant he sort of became our unofficial "plant man" and he loved it. He got such a buzz out of this that he set up a little stall outside the entrance to the public living room and handed out little plants in pots to anyone who looked like they needed a lift. After a while someone at the library got to hear about him and his plants and, quite amazingly, they asked him to tend their gardens, all the grass verges and flower beds circling the grand, Victorian library. This was a request which Colin received as if he had won the lottery. He told everyone he was the Library's head gardener and that felt good. However, Colin still had dark days where he just closed up and felt terribly down and today was one of them.

After about ten minutes I could tell Colin had decided to deploy his usual barrage of "Dad" jokes on Beverley. I had to run some errands that day but I could hear the pair of them laughing as I left. When I returned that afternoon I found Beverley had taken off her blood-stained hoodie and was wearing an apron and taking orders for teas and coffees from everyone in the public living room.

There should be more places like this.

Places you can go when you can just walk straight into helping someone else when you have a rough day yourself. Why? Because it's magic. What happened between Beverley and Colin is a counter-intuitive transaction but one that completely altered how I see "charity work" when I first encountered it properly. Something so normal and yet also so radical that the system ensures there is no space for it. It challenges the system's franchise over suffering; the last thing the system wants is people realising they have the power themselves to look out for each other and that these tiny, seemingly inconsequential moments of mutuality can actually make all the difference. People can help themselves?! Whaaaat?!! So the system smothers everything in policies and makes such an act a "safeguarding" issue or other tension-inducing words that scare the crap out of everyone and stop anything good and human from happening.

And so this vibe is missing in most places you go in times of trouble. We live in a world where there must always be a benefactor and a beneficiary in strictly observed roles. Those who receive help and those who give it. I could start telling you what the 1834 Poor Laws did to our notions of "deserving and undeserving poor" or give you my best rant about Social Darwinism and how enthralled the human race became with Greco-Roman systems of hierarchy versus collaborative, mutual associational life as espoused by Pyotr Kropotkin around about the same time as Darwin ... but then you might start looking for an exit so I'll move on and keep this rooted in the stories of people I met (Ok so I actually give in and have this rant in a few chapters time so just skip it if you want!).

That day in the library I just asked Beverley to come out of her problems for a moment and consider somebody else. Callous you might think, when the woman had just gone through horrific trauma in her own home. Yet it gave her temporary relief and took her out of that tunnel vision of pain she had descended into. All I said was six words.

"Can you do me a favour?"

These six words convey gigantic, life-altering concepts without realising it. It tells someone that ...

... they are trusted ...

... they have value ...

... they belong here ...

... and maybe other people don't have all the answers ...

... and it shows them that maybe it's OK to be a bit rubbish and ask for help sometimes. I didn't ask those teenagers in Liverpool to do me a favour with that furniture, but I think it worked that way all the same. They had something to do, it felt good loading the van for me and they could see how grateful I was. Truth is, I was knackered and I did need their help that day. They knew they'd done something for me, but then the chocolates told me their act of kindness was returning the favour of the public living room. It was a mutual thing, we were doing something for each other.

Looking out for others when we are the ones struggling seems to lift us up and out of our problems. It's another of Camerados' 6 principles and that's just because I've seen this work like absolute magic so many times over 30 years working with people who have all sorts of tough lives and situations. Being as so many people tell me that this is counter-intuitive and doesn't make sense to them, I feel I have to use a couple more stories to illustrate it.

Back in the days when I ran a homeless charity I met a fella rocking back and forwards on a chair in one of our day centres. He had bloodshot eyes from crying and a scar on his forehead from where he was stabbed in the park trying to break up a fight. He was sleeping in that park because his wife had changed the locks on their house the second time that he'd come out of rehab. She wouldn't let him see the kids. Last he heard she'd actually moved to Cornwall. He was at the end, didn't see a future; his next step, so he told me, was to summon up the courage to end it all. Somewhere in the conversation he told me that he'd been a painter and decorator so I asked him what he thought I could do to make my drab day centre a little nicer. I hadn't a clue and was rubbish at all that kind of thing (totally true) so needed his advice. He walked me round every room telling me what we could do. He put his hand on my shoulder, smiled and told me to stop worrying, that we could figure it out. He became animated about colour, about where we'd get the paint from, we laughed at my inept suggestions and we put the kettle on in order to properly weigh up the scale of the impending redecoration he had in mind. I'm not saying the whole arc of the fella's life changed that afternoon but he didn't want to kill himself anymore. The dynamic changed in an instant. Somehow that asking for his advice, a favour, it re-wired his brain from the tunnel of hell he was in, at least in that moment.

I was walking down my own street a couple of years back and a teaching assistant from my son's primary school stopped me and was keen to tell me that she'd applied this Camerado principle and it had worked wonders in her classroom. There was a young girl in Year 5 who was very active, loud and struggled to get through the day without disrupting the class every 10 or 20 minutes and it was wearing everyone out, including the girl herself. So one day she asked the girl to help her sort the books in the classroom, she became the class book monitor, the librarian if you will. After that the girl arrived early for school every day and sorted out the book corner. It now looks really nice and organised and the noisy disruption has completely stopped.

This might not be a magic wand every time but in situations where I haven't seen a possibility for progress it has rarely let me down.

LOCHGILPHEAD

Lochgilphead is a small town of around 2,000 people situated at the end of Loch Gilp, an offshoot of the famous oyster waters of Loch Fyne in Argyll & Bute. It's about two hours west of Glasgow with scenery so breathtakingly beautiful – with its hillsides showing off all the greens, all the browns and every purple kind of heather you could dream up alongside lochs and sea lochs bubbling, glistening and sparkling in the sun – that my 12 year old son, along for the ride, keeps telling me off for shouting. It's impossible not to punctuate our van drive around the many turns that follow the shore of the lake without involuntary cries of "GOOD GOD will you look at THAT" and after the umpteenth image of complete heaven "Oh come on that's enough, this is getting RIDICULOUS". Scotland can do this to you.

We didn't have to put the furniture on the pavement in Lochgilphead because they'd already done it. It turns out that their regular public living room goes outside onto the streets when the sun is shining. As everyone knows, the sun always shines in Scotland so they are finding themselves doing this a LOT! Not so much, so we felt lucky to be there on a day of sun and outdoor tea and cakes.

The Snowdrop Centre is for people affected by neurological and other long term conditions, as well as being a centre for anyone feeling socially isolated. Although public living rooms are run by whoever wanders in them in a mutual, leaderless way, they get started because a small group of folk or sometimes one individual gives a damn and wants to get something going in their street or neighbourhood. In Lochgilphead that's Karen, one of those irrepressibly positive, can-do people who help communities be heard, take action, and have power over their lives. Every neighbourhood needs a Karen. In fact, if every single community in the world had a Karen and we supported, funded and gave their Karen the freedom to do their thing we would have an astronomically better world than we do. But we don't tend to do that because top-down, hierarchical, "don't trust the locals", Government-knows-best societies are working so well for us! Sorry accidental rant there, it's involuntary sometimes, I'll rein it in.

As I'm talking to one woman opposite me I notice someone over her shoulder, a woman stood motionless on the other side of the street. She's wearing jeans and a white jogging top, her hair in bunches and she's clutching her bag and staring in our direction. She's watching a small boy who appears beside us, running. He gets to a table nearby that holds crates full of free food bank food – bread, some vegetables and a few tins. He collects some items then without looking at us turns and runs back across the street to his mum, the woman staring at him, and she shoves the items in her bag and quickly scurries on, yanking the boy's hand as she goes, not looking back at us. "Aye there's a lot of shame surrounding food banks," says Karen, the centre manager, as she cradles her mug of tea, "which is why we started doing the public living room so folk could just come for a cuppa without the stigma attached to the food bank."

The mix of people always makes for great, unlikely topics of conversation. Next to a few elderly retired women sits a young man called Philip. He is very interested in finding out everything about everyone and asks me quick-fire questions ranging from sport to food to work to light entertainment to friendships. "What's your favourite TV programme from your childhood?"; "Do you believe the moon landing was real?"; "What colour fizzy drink do you prefer?". It's a very condensed and efficient way to have a conversation, and build up a profile of someone. I ask him if he works for the CIA but he reassures me it's just how he likes to talk.

A woman who runs a local housing association tells me that every morning she comes into work she checks on her computer the output of electricity from the two windmills on the coast, facing out to the Atlantic. I ask her if she's a gigantic renewable energy nerd and she responds "yes!" but tells me why. These windmills belong to the housing association and generate power and money for the community. Every time they sell energy back to the grid a grant – thousands of pounds – goes back to local organisations and initiatives. "This is how the world should work," I say. "Exactly and it is working very well thank you very much here in Argyll and

Bute!" she says proudly. "She does love her windmills," says Karen. "Oh she does," says the woman opposite. "I love a windmill," says another woman. "What's your favourite muppet?" says Philip.

On the rare occasion the weather isn't good in Scotland, Karen and some locals set up the public living room inside the centre and project a video of a log burning fire on the wall to make it cosy! "The only problem with those days is that a lot of folk won't turn the handle on the door and step inside to a room full of strangers. One fella only comes when we're outside." Karen is talking about a chap who moved here for a job as a chef in a nearby hotel. He doesn't know anybody. Karen tells me this is common in the hospitality industry, especially in Scotland because a lot of the hotels are in remote, rural places where there's plenty of breathtaking natural beauty but also life-taking isolation. "Hotel staff travel from place to place for work, their shifts are often long and hard. Outside of that they just want to sleep. It's hard to build a community of friends that way." Then to my surprise, and Karen's, the chef turns up as we're sitting there and everyone gives him the warmest welcome. A lovely gentle, quiet chap with a mane of silver hair he perches on the edge of the sofa and lets the conversation happen around him, happy if it comes to him but just as happy if it doesn't. He chats to us for a while, about his hometown in France, the kitchen staff he despairs of, the need to be very careful when shucking oysters. I thought as I talked to him that not all chefs are Gordon Ramsay shouting types, but then perhaps he's different on his working days? Something told me not. When the day ended he was kind and helped me put my furniture back in the van.

I heard much later that he had gone through some very difficult times but in the midst of them, late at night, he'd reached out and texted the only set of people he knew: Karen and the Camerados in the local public living room.

WHEN HUMANS ORGANISE

The idea that being organised can cause more harm than good

Whatever you do, don't organise too much.

We can't help ourselves, you see. All of us. The moment we decide to do something, any kind of project, we have to *organise*. That's a good thing surely? Well yes but it brings all kinds of peril, peril we almost never acknowledge. When we organise we become obsessed with neatness and efficiency as if these are always good things. I hear some of you shouting at the page "BUT THEY ARE!". But humans aren't efficient, they are messy as hell. So your perfect organisation is going to struggle to be fit for humans.

When we organise we systemise *and so we* dehumanise.

Systems are useful for sure; processes can help keep the emotional out of work sometimes, they regulate for the messy humans involved. You can point to a process and people won't hate you; you're just following the process. However, these systems can also restrict, imprison, blunt people's creativity, refuse to adapt and cause real harm.

Like the whole thing around opening hours. I've worked with so many services that effectively say, "Could you please have your mental health breakdown between 9.30am and 4.30am?". The telephone operator who

99

has to tell clients, "I'm sorry but you have to come into the clinic if you want help with your mobility." The noticeboard that unthinkingly announces: "Never been able to read, write or recognise numbers? Literacy and numeracy class is on Wednesdays at 4–6pm." Have a think about that.

We forget humans are involved. We do things that suit our staffing rota, our funder requirements, we serve the system not the human.

Also when we over-organise we don't leave space for others.

Galvanising people isn't about having it all mapped out, it's about standing in front of a room and saying, "I need your help!"

It's Blackpool in the early days of Camerados, back when our team created all the public living rooms ourselves and were learning about what made them tick. I am standing in the beautiful library, high windows with stained glass, walls edged with frilly cornices, and in front of me is a crowd of local people who answered the call to come along and have pizza.

Sat there in Blackpool is a crazy mix of people: nurses from the hospital, artists from the bohemian quarter, shop owners from the neighbourhood, residents from the local rehab and hostel, council employees..

"Where are you getting all this furniture from?" shouts someone in the crowd.

"I have no idea really, any thoughts?" I say.

Silence. There's a general feeling in the air that "this guy doesn't know what he's doing". I look like I mean it. I do.

"I've got a sofa I don't need, you can have that," says a woman in the front row.

"Thanks, that's great."

"Did you say you needed a piano?" says an old guy at the very back of the room.

"Yep, it would be great for creating a nice vibe I think," I say.

"Ok, I've got one in my shop," he says. Then a fella across the back of the room from him leans back on his chair and starts talking to him. I only hear the end of the conversation when the guy says, "Tuesday OK for you?" Turns out the other guy owns a big van and they've just arranged to collect the piano and bring it here. I'm not even involved in the planning. If I'd had a "piano" column in my Excel spreadsheet I would have missed out on that bit of community, people powered magic.

Another thing happens when we over organise. We shout.

If you over-organise then you are seeking some sort of perfection. The problem is that on Day One of almost any project humans turn up and so the chances for perfection go out the window. You poured your heart into thinking of every last detail for your party, your event, whatever, and now you are standing in the kitchen shouting at someone because it's not what you intended. The pursuit of order and perfection can only really result in somebody somewhere shouting in the kitchen. It just drives the wrong behaviours and makes people act poorly and feel horrible about themselves ultimately. We get guilt, compulsion, a general feeling that you're always failing because you never achieve perfection. Look at the Catholic church, it doesn't end well (I speak as a bad, lapsed Catholic).

This is why I did, in fact, invent a rule. A rule?! Yep, stay with me here. We made a book. It goes in the box that people get when they want to make a public living room in their neighbourhood. I was banned from the meetings that made the book in the end because I had too much to say and the book had to be short and simple. I do bang on a bit. As they were throwing me out the door I jammed my foot in the gap and made one request before it squashed my shoe leather. Whatever they put in there, the only thing I would die in a ditch to keep would be this one rule. So here it is. The rule.

"When you set out to do something, ANYTHING, that involves humans, always be a little bit crap."

Inspiring isn't it!

So important though. If we are imperfect then it gives others permission to be the same. It creates a relaxed atmosphere where humans can be gloriously imperfect. Nothing turns people away more than the shouty person in the kitchen. That person has been me on many occasions. I hide behind things like, "It's because I care so much". Nope, in that instance I care about nothing but me and what I want to happen! Observe the rule of being a bit crap in all that we do and you will keep it *human*.

Don't miss the chapter further on about this very subject – it's called "We're all a bit shit sometimes". If you take nothing else away from this book please take away that thought!

Public living rooms
from around the world

Middlesbrough

PORT TALBOT

Imagine the film *Blade Runner* had been made by Ken Loach. Welcome to Port Talbot. Sea on one side, mountains on the other; it should be stunningly beautiful, but unfortunately they decided to stick a smoke-belching, metropolis of a steelworks on the shore and then pile-drive a motorway through the middle of the houses in the town. Concrete legs walk over the rooftops of houses propping up the carriageways as trucks and cars hurriedly bypass the town to and from west Wales. A mountain brook is carefully walled off from view as it descends the mountains, under the M4, passes lines of terraced houses, a high street of vape shops and cafés and ends up under the Tesco's and presumably makes it to the sea, which nobody can see anymore.

So before I get lynched by Michael Sheen and anyone else from Port Talbot, I must say that the fact this is the scene that greets you says so much about the greatness of the people here that they remain so welcoming, seemingly happy and always up for a chat. Richard Burton and Anthony Hopkins came from here too so there's something in the air evidently – probably hydrogen sulphide – and when you talk to folk they are proud of being from Port Talbot. I found that to be the case anyway.

Graeme and Harry were tucking into a fry-up at the caff opposite our public living room. I followed them there not just because I love a British Caff, but because they'd stood observing and commenting on the public living room for the preceding half hour and we now carried on our conversation over sausage, egg and chips. Harry was at great pains to tell me that his lifelong friend Graeme had started off working on the furnaces at the steelworks but someone had spotted potential in him. He took a bunch of courses and ended up at University. He returned to the Steelworks in a more senior engineering position and all the lads were proud of him. Graeme brushed this aside with a hand that held the brown sauce and started to give me his view on the future of the plant. This was a sore topic today. We had arrived in Port Talbot one week after the announcement of 2,800 job losses. The company, Tata Steel, had decided to decommission the two furnaces and move the plant to a different, supposedly more Green form of steel production. Graeme had been writing to the Chief Exec with his thoughts but the replies had dried up. Shame, because the level of detail and insight in what Graeme was outlining seemed to be worth listening to. It made me wonder how many industries have pensioned off such wisdom, wisdom that perhaps could have saved them had they listened.

Halfway through the day a spaceman turned up. He kept his helmet on, presumably worried about the air quality, but talked to me as we played Connect Four. Sadly, it turned out that his astronaut credentials were minimal and he was wearing the suit to cause a stir and advertise a local music festival coming up that summer. He told me he had a kinship with what we were doing because people need things to cheer them up in hard times and he felt their event always went down well because when news is bad and times are tough sometimes you just need to dance in a field and let our hair down. I allowed the phrase "bread and circuses" to roll around my head but landed on agreement.

As we sat there a man wandered up to us holding a very tiny sausage dog on his lead. He had a lovely low voice and a three-day stubble. He gave us an impromptu lecture on the history of the town and how beautiful it used to be with funfairs on the beach, walks up the mountains etc. He didn't blink twice that he was giving this lecture to a spaceman; he was too passionate about how things used to be. He told us how the old firms used to invest in the town and build churches, schools and whatnot. He pointed at the beautiful derelict church hall behind us and regaled us of all the fine concerts that used to happen there. The spaceman piped up: "The police busted open the basement of that church not long ago and found one of the biggest weed factories in south Wales." The man just nodded and said, "Times have changed that's for sure."

Unsurprisingly everyone you talked to had some sort of connection to the steel works. One woman worked at the local women's refuge and told us that she expected to have a lot more customers now the news had hit of the plant closing. She had a number of relatives involved in the plant, including a daughter-in-law in a senior executive position. The talks around the kitchen table were animated, she had said, with competing agendas from climate change to jobs to the welfare of their community. She told me she'd love her refuge to run a public living room so they could spend time with more than just the victims of domestic violence but the people who lived in the houses around those victims and most of all men who might be, or have the potential to be, the perpetrators too. If they chatted more maybe they'd all hear stories that illuminated the impacts of their own and their communities actions more.

As I left the town I have to be honest and say the whole day left a scar on me. I was angry. Port Talbot seemed to me to be the starkest example of people and a community coming last to commerce and politics. Of course it's naive – I know that the steelworks brought jobs and gave these folk a livelihood – but just looking down on the town from the hill as you leave it feels like the people are left with the scraps, houses tucked into places left by sprawling factories and motorways. Places to meet, eat or play with your kids ... I just didn't see them. Money first, people last. Not a place built for humans. The *Bladerunner* comparison fits.

CRAP LIVES MATTER

The idea that there is a form of discrimination we never talk about

Some people have crap lives and to make it worse society hates them for it.

You listen to some people's stories and think they must have walked under a forest of ladders. I think there needs to be more awareness of these people and quite a lot more tolerance and understanding towards them. There are many "isms" we have come to acknowledge that exist in our world, pernicious prejudices that fuel our unconscious bias towards certain sections of society. I would like to offer up that "Crapism" could be added.

I've met a great deal of these people over the years because a lot of them ended up in the many hostels, refuges or rehabs that I used to run. These are not people in war zones, facing famine, suffering torture or whatever untold horror exists in some parts of the world; for those people there is unlikely to be any debate that we should be concerned about their welfare (whether we do anything about it is another matter). No, the people I'm talking about are those people who do not have our concern, who have no identifiable, extinguishable feature that calls upon our sympathy. They're not a child with cancer, not a victim of a crime or life-altering accident. They just haven't coped very well with life.

So they've made some bad choices, had some bad luck, most commonly in my experience they've just had a series of events in their life which knocked them down one path rather than another until they ended up in a labyrinth of problems where every turn seems to trigger a opportunity for unsound choices and decisions, reactions and overreactions, that just lead further into a downward spiral of catastrophe, and make it almost impossible to navigate the world or just a single day. Often it started out with them saying something a bit stupid and went from there. Honestly, you'd be astonished at the ludicrously arbitrary nature of people's mishaps and hard lives. Not only do they not have our concern but they tend to get the full weight of society's judgement. "It's their own doing," we say, as if saying or thinking that ever made anything better.

The notion that some people are deserving and undeserving of our support is not new. It feels like if we scratch beneath the surface of many people's views today we find this "undeserving" prejudice embedded pretty deep inside people's consciousness. Where does it come from? Though I'm sure there was always a caveman kicked out of the cave for not achieving his quota of mammoth kills, the idea seems to have taken root in the establishment in relatively modern times throughout the 1800s. It's likely that it started with a very odd clergyman in the parish of Wotton, Surrey.

The curate Thomas Malthus wrote a publication in 1798 called "An Essay on the Principle of Population" and in it he put forward the theory that the growth of population would always outstrip the production of food and resources to support it and therefore our species was doomed if we kept supporting the poor. Hold on, this fella got a gig as a vicar? Mind you, the things Thomas found helpful to solve this conundrum, to level the population – war, famine, pestilence etc. – they do all turn up on horseback in the *Book of Revelations* so perhaps his profession is not entirely surprising. As shocking as this view is, it caught on and became hugely influential a few decades later in a landmark bit of legislation called The Poor Law Amendment Act in 1834.

Alarmed by the cost of poor relief, and short of cash due to poor harvests, the Whig Government used Malthus' philosophy to justify a policy that removed relief from the poor unless they entered workhouses. It was a pernicious bit of legislation predicated on the idea that if we make the provision of welfare unpleasant then it will act as a deterrent to people seeking and using it. Significantly though, this act is the first time we hear about this distinction of "deserving and undeserving poor". The "deserving" became poor through no fault of their own – illness, age etc. – while the "undeserving" were essentially just seen as lazy and feckless. Undeserving people can just die off and help us all out.

Amazingly this got a lot of traction. And then things got really serious, thanks to a lot of guys who came along in the second half of the century and all of whom, as it happens, rocked a serious amount of pretty wild facial hair. Herbert Spencer was a bit of a rockstar philosopher – yep radical sideburns – and building on Malthus he coined the famous phrase "Survival of the fittest". Much to the delight of Spencer, however, his musings were about to become scientific fact thanks to the arrival of the man of his age, the biggest beardy of them all, Charles Darwin. Darwin's "natural selection" idea – that the stronger species survive – was a fantastic biological justification of Malthus and Spencer. Many defenders of Darwin say that Spencer mangled his ideas and applying natural selection to humans and society was never what he intended. However, sorry folks, but Darwin used the "Survival of the fittest" phrase himself in the fifth edition of *The Origin of the Species* in 1869 in an obvious nod to Spencer, who he apparently greatly admired. This "Social Darwinism" – as it became known much later – seems to have used the cloak of science to justify deeply unpleasant views about the fate of those who have a harder time in life.

As if this wasn't bad enough, Darwin's cousin, Francis Galton – terrifically hairy sidies – took it further into much darker territory. Galton was a Victorian polymath who produced the first weather map, carried out experiments on the power of prayer and – you gotta love him for this – looked into how to make the perfect cup of tea. He is, however, also the father of eugenics, having invented the term, and we have to love him quite a bit less for that. Eugenics proposed that the human species could be "improved" by selective mating of people with "higher characteristics". The disabled and poor must be weeded out of the population and aristocrats and smart folk should interbreed to produce a better class of human species. Profoundly classist, racist and utterly abhorrent, eugenics has of course been derided and discredited not least because of its adoption many years later by the Nazis as a justification for their diabolical actions.

So if the work of all these hirsute Victorians has been discredited and derided, why bother to mention it? Well because I'm not sure it's entirely disappeared. I think it lives under the covers of our thinking to this day, simmering under prejudices modified for more modern palatable tastes, revealing itself occasionally in the careless rabble rousing of populist politicians on all sides of the political spectrum. Some want to make their country "great again" or "get back control" mostly by weeding out races who don't belong or cutting support for the undeserving. Others on the other side of the political spectrum refer to these people as "the deplorables" and mock their ignorant ways on comedy shows or scream "fascist scum" phrases at anti-fascist rallies, as well as other slogans that do nothing to build bridges. When politicians use language like "strivers not skivers" or "shirkers, not workers" (phrases used by right- and left-wing parties, respectively) the echoes of 1834's parliament and of Social Darwinism are alive and well. When you say "I don't give to beggars because they'll only spend it on drugs" it's there too. What do you know about that person's life except what you have cobbled together from the prejudices that informed the likes of Frances Galton, who presumably expected the breeding aristocrats to create far more superior choices than the guy in your doorway? Does that feel uncomfortable for you right now? It should. We judge people whose lives we haven't lived and cannot fathom and use lazy, yet horrific, logic to justify our actions.

So I offer you the idea of "Crapism". Many of us cannot understand how it feels to be on the receiving end of racism. Some of us cannot understand the million tiny prejudices that a woman feels in a single day. People with disabilities, the trans community, refugees, immigrants, there is a long list of injustices and "isms" towards people with whom we can try to empathise but unless you are part of that community you can never fully understand how it feels. But with "Crapism" we can all understand.

Public living rooms
from around the world
Freetown
Sierra Leone

THIS IS A PUBLIC LIVING ROOM.
ALL WELCOME COME ON IN!

GLASGOW

BRIDGETON CROSS

I'm on the street in Bridgeton Cross, Glasgow, and there's a red-faced elderly woman spitting the words "Step back" at me with her hand raised in anger. In case the sands of time have covered up this memory for you, dear reader, this happened when the pandemic was still a thing, even if the world was starting to recover and get back to some normality at this point. The woman's reaction is a bit of a shocking start to my day, not least because I'm here with my pavement public living room to promote human connection. It's my own fault. She asked me why there was a sofa and some armchairs on the pavement and I instinctively walked towards her to answer. Had I not filled her with fear she might have appreciated what I was doing, but now she doesn't want to hear anything from me because, by my walking towards her and reducing the social distance between us she feels that I'm putting her life at risk. Which is pretty extraordinary. Yep, the pandemic really set us back on the whole social connection piece.

Two local women in raincoats carrying bags of shopping come over to me and look at the public living room in the middle of the street and say, "Is this a warrant sale? They'll put your name in the window!" They laugh and wander off. I found out later from another visitor that, back in the day when landlords evicted you in Glasgow, they'd bring all of your furniture out into the street and sell it in front of everyone. Also, local shops would put your name in the window so people knew you weren't good for credit. People still use that expression around here, "I'll put your name in the window!" if you are late with a debt. Apparently the practice of warrant sales was only banned by the council in the 2000s. No wonder people isolate themselves if this is how we shame those who are struggling.

Today gave me some hope, though. A local resident who sat on my sofa realised the fella who wandered by was the local councillor she'd been wanting to talk to. I could sense he'd been "nabbed" and it was delicious to watch. However, other local power brokers also loved this chance to meet folk in this unfiltered way and chat, face to face. Susan Aktemel, founder of the ethical lettings agency Homes for Good is one. She was with us because her organisation hosts a regular public living room nearby every Thursday and I loved that here she was on a wet Wednesday just hanging out with us on the sofa in the street.

As I did with Jess in Hastings, I find myself being uncomfortable around Susan sometimes because she's so normal when she's chatting to you and the whole time you're thinking: "I want to tell everyone here that you're not normal, you're actually bloody amazing cos you've done insanely re-markable things that nobody else has even thought of doing." It's as if you find yourself on a bus sat opposite Neil Armstrong or Ruth Bader Gins-burg and they're casually eating a Mars bar and nobody notices. Anyway, Susan notices a woman carrying a Pyrex dish down the street and she offers her an armchair for a chat. A conversation about apple crumble leads to a realisation that the woman lived in one of Susan's properties and actually they'd been meaning to catch up about an issue with her tenancy. Susan is relishing this and there is a quality to their chat that I just don't think would have happened had the meeting been arranged and in a meeting room. At another point, six Ukrainian refugees turn up. Six women wonderfully coiffured whose stylish clothes and impeccable makeup challenge my stereotypical idea of the word "refugee". They take up residence in the public living room as if it's the most natural place in the world to put a sofa for them to sit on – I suppose they have fled war, which is kind of more outrageous and noteworthy – and the chats flow freely about their children's schooling, ideas for winter recipes (Borscht takes time, apparently I'm rushing it), the state of global politics and a suggestion that a public living room is a great way to meet men! Amidst raucous laughter they have decided Camerados needs a tie-in with Tinder.

After a while, Susan has to get back to work and takes her intergalactic, Mars bar self off down the very drab, normal street. This acts as a cue for the Ukrainian women to go too and to their great amusement they make me air kiss them farewell. It grows quiet when they all leave. There's that sound of people not being there anymore and I'm a bit lonely for the next half hour. Until Billy and Stuart happen along. They are two local boys who have lived and worked in Bridgeton all their life. Billy is bit Bill Nighy, Stuart more of a William Shatner. They both break into song about the famous Mermaid Bar that used to be situated opposite where we're sitting and they tell me about 33 pubs on the Kilmarnock Road that are all gone now. However, their animated banter goes up a notch when telling me about a structure that stands about 100 feet from us – the Bridgeton Umbrella. This octagonal cast iron shelter has been a public meeting place since 1894 and is the most iconic symbol of the area. However, anger ripples through the veins on Billy's face when he tells me the Umbrella is being taken away to be restored. He doesn't like the fact it's being removed at all (despite the fact another passing fella tells me it's definitely coming back and will be in even better condition). Billy is not convinced. "Some say if that disnae come back here then we'll torch the Olympia building!" The Olympia building is the symbol of the new regeneration in the neighbourhood as it is the offices of the company leading the changes. It struck me that in our time together, although Billy has chatted to me about how hard times are, locally he's more angry about a dilapidated bit of iron that serves absolutely no purpose anymore. It doesn't feed him, doesn't pay his heating bills, doesn't make his area better. Or does it? It's about an idea very dear to Billy though he never says it explicitly. The idea of community, a place and its people. Right now it's all they've got. "They're putting padlocks on the Lurpak in my corner shop," Billy says. "It's no cheap nowadays, It's six quid or thereabouts! For butter man!"

Sandra knows this. She runs the café called Sucre where we've been buying our coffees to stay warm today. "Everything's gone up – butter, milk, cheese – and I cannae pass those costs onto my customers cos they haven't got the money, they won't come in. But you see all the big café chains in the West End? Their prices are double mine. Mind you, they're empty right now cos folk are not going out." We talk about what that means. It doesn't seem a big deal to not go out for a coffee with a pal, but it's those coffee meet ups where people notice how each other's doing, check in, cajole each other along, get ideas. Sandra agrees that conversation illuminates things for us about ourselves, generates ideas and also just makes us feel like it's all going to be OK. "We need that," says Billy, looking forlornly into the distance at his crappy iron umbrella thing sat in the middle of a drab, unremarkable square, "of course we need that, always have."

WHAT IS YOUR CONFIDENCE POLICY?

The idea that the creation of "confidence" gets so little attention and yet we can't do anything without it.

I asked this question recently to a couple of Governors at the comprehensive school that my sons attend. "What is your confidence policy?".

They are lovely fellas but they looked at me as if I was mad. The school had just introduced a pretty aggressive Uniform policy, they had an Attendance policy, a Behaviour policy and so on ... it just seemed a bit pointless unless they also had a confidence policy being as the lack of confidence often leads to non-attendance at school, bad behaviour etc. Also I don't think any teacher would argue against confidence being a massive driver in children achieving success at school. So where is it in the day-to-day? Is it ever mentioned? And how much is confidence bashed and jostled by the relentless focus on measuring every pupil's "success", predicting grades, colour coding behaviour? Things that inevitably damage, as much as encourage, success. Frankly most kids I speak to are either freaked out or fed up by all that stuff.

But how do you achieve confidence?

Well I'm sure there are far more scholarly places to go for that answer but, being as this book is purely based on my experience of working with people with tough lives, all I can offer you is that it seems to me to be a mix of encouragement, trust and knowing someone has your back. And maybe a little more encouragement. And a touch more.

A surgeon wandered into a public living room that was in the atrium of a hospital in Blackpool once and said, "I've heard about this place and I think I need it today." He proceeded to talk about how he wasn't really coping today. A surgeon! Surely one of the last bastions of absolute power and total confidence one might assume. A patient from one of the wards was sitting there in her pink terry-towelling dressing gown and pyjamas and she looked at the surgeon and said, "Do you need a hug, love?". He laughed and said that would be great and everyone in the public living room smiled as she cuddled the tall surgeon who was standing there in his scrubs. They chatted for a while until the surgeon stood up and said, "Right, that's just what I needed, I best get back, I've got an operation this afternoon."

I love that story because it's not often that the power dynamic of patient and surgeon is flipped like that. It shows that anyone can have a rough time and need a confidence boost and that this boost can come from anyone. I also love how transitory the relationship was, it didn't take long and it wasn't a big commitment.

Some doctors have crappy lives. Nurses, teachers, lawyers ... all the folk we're supposed to think have it nailed, nobody is excused from it. Often the people in the most "capable" jobs suffer from the fact they have to conceal the fact they don't feel remotely capable inside themselves. The need to always be achieving, always caring or always be right; this can turn you inside out, but you're not allowed help, sympathy or a time-out because you should be grateful for the great job you have. In a survey in 2024 by the British Medical Association, 80% of doctors said they were at "high/very high risk of burnout" and 27% of them reported being diagnosed with a mental health condition at some point in their life. Despite these high figures, only 53% of the doctors had sought support. Why is that? Did they feel they would be judged, looked down upon for not coping? [4]

4   *Caring for the mental health of the medical workforce*, https://www.bma.org.uk/media/cksh-vkzc/bma-mental-health-survey-report-september-2024.pdf

It's just a fact that if you're not coping you are treated differently. Even people very light on the scale of "crapism" experience prejudice too. I would include myself and many of you reading this because I'm sure we are lightly mocked at least a few times every week, or maybe even every day, for some minor shortfall in our ability. Often that takes a tiny microscopic chip off our confidence cheese, that big block of cheese at the centre of our being from which everything we do radiates and takes its energy and motivation. "Is that the worst thing to happen, though, snowflake?" I hear you ask in your best Piers Morgan voice. "Somebody knocks you, oh dear, boo hoo." Well if you're not in a good place or, like many of us, hold vast reservoirs of self doubt in our subconscious then those knocks add up and change the shape of us. We cannot do anything without that damn confidence cheese, and those little seemingly manageable microscopic knocks take chunk after chunk out of it.

Yet how many schools, colleges, workplaces spend their day concerned about it?

Confidence is the bedrock on which everything rises or falls yet we happily knock it about and watch it crumble and spend precious little time attending to it, talking about it, doing things to look after it. Most of us muddle through with wonky looking cheese and still get by OK, especially if we started life with a bigger block of cheese than others. Those of us who are white privileged men for instance. Yep, our cheese started out the size of Wyoming. However, some people start with tiny blobs of cheddar and then have it toasted to shit. It's in tiny molten bits all over the place so that the confidence to do anything is going to be very tricky. They tend to have very tough lives and people with big cheese find it hard to understand this and connect with them. So it's so much easier to resort to "crapism" and judge them and give them a wide berth.

I have this ritual every Christmas Eve, I watch the film "It's a wonderful Life" as I'm wrapping presents. The film's hero, George Bailey, played by James Stewart, gets to see how his world would look had he never been born. Could you imagine what might happen if we all had a chance to see what the world would be like when we don't give each other any trust and encouragement and people lack confidence in themselves? Then I had a horrible thought, what if that's what we've already got.

CUMNOCK

Crayon green hillsides rolled down from plump cloudy skies as we arrived on the outskirts of town, but looking up we saw that sat atop them were line after line of severe looking, uniformly spaced grey houses and the overall effect was as if Stalin had invaded Trumpton.

I was with my colleague Catherine. We entered a pretty drab looking community centre and were directed to a room where a women's group was sitting silently listening to a facilitator who'd obviously just carried out a collage-making workshop involving cut outs from catalogues, presumably about their hopes and fears. Everyone looked a bit depressed, wearing sweatpants and wishing they were at home, so I didn't hold out much hope that they'd be up for the pavement shenanigans we had in mind. Catherine was a passionate believer in getting adults to remember how to play and she wanted to get them dancing in the street wearing giant silk underpants. I looked at her and thought of a clown at a funeral.

I couldn't have been more wrong. When we hit town and put the sofas outside Farmfoods by a main road, the women came alive. They didn't sit down in the public living room, they grabbed the giant underpants, put them straight on, cackling and hooting as they did so, and started pulling in passersby to join in. Cars pipped and waved and people crossed the street.

Nicola, who was the ringleader, seemed to know everybody in the town. She has a personal story that would make the rest of us lock the door and never leave the house again, yet here she was dancing around the street flirting with car drivers who pipped at her and waved.

An elderly lady turned up to chat to Nicola. She told me that she was psychic and could speak with the dead. She wouldn't mind so much except her dead husband never shut up. She'd recently been broken into and had an idea who it was. She asked her husband but he hadn't seen anything. Useless.

She was telling me this when a woman came out of the Poundshop opposite and made a beeline for us. It was her daughter's 18th birthday and she didn't have anything special for her and no money to get it anyway. She started crying, and the woman who talked to dead people comforted her, putting her arm around her in a motherly way. The woman clutched some brightly coloured ribbons in her hand and shook with tears about what a rubbish mum she was. Nicola and the other women from the public living room came over and told her not to be daft. "Your daughter has you on her birthday, a mum who loves her, and that's enough." "Aye, how many folk can say that round here, a mum who loves them," they laughed, and so did the woman. We chatted a little longer with her and she wiped her eyes, straightened her coat, gave the psychic woman a kiss on the cheek and wandered off.

The dancing in pants had drawn a crowd. Suddenly the schools emptied and teenagers invaded our pavement public living room. Far from being embarrassed, the pants were handed round and people were busting moves with passing shoppers. I went to Greggs for supplies and filled a bag full of steak bakes and sausage rolls. When I went to pay, the staff said there was no charge but they wouldn't mind a go with our pants.

A teenager wandered up later in the afternoon and one of the women gave him a big hug. She was his mum. He was a big hulk of a lad with a round face and a sweet smile. He was a cheerful soul and had an apprenticeship at a nearby garage. We talked about engines and I faked knowledge of cars to be honest. After he left his mum told me he'd been through a lot. He'd come home and found his dad swinging from a light in the hall, trying to hang himself. It had just happened and the boy reacted quickly, propping up his dad so he didn't choke to death. He called 999 and an ambulance came. The dad died later though.

You wouldn't put 'dancing in pants' alongside stories like that. Yet what would you put beside it?

It reminded me of a man who wandered into a public living room and played Connect Four with us for hours. He suddenly said "I was wandering up and down this street all morning looking for somewhere to kill myself, but you know what? I'd forgotten how much I love Connect Four. So I don't think I'll do it today." Sometimes it's something tiny, something silly that can just nudge you out of harm's way and back to feeling human and hopeful.

Public living rooms
from around the world

Cumnock

BIG PANTS ARE BETTER THAN A MOLOTOV COCKTAIL

The idea that being silly can beat tyranny

One day in 2017 I sat in the backroom of a pub in Colchester sharing a pint of bitter and a Scotch egg with a man who brings down dictators for a living.

His name is Srdja Popovic, a Serbian revolutionary who played a leading role in ending the violent reign of Slobodan Milosevic. He is charismatic and hugely personable and loves Monty Python. He now runs an organisation called CANVAS, the Centre for Applied Non Violent Actions and Strategies, who quite literally advises people on how to use non-violent methods to take on the totalitarian regimes under which they live. The subtitle of his book *Blueprint for Revolution*[5] is "How to use Rice pudding, Lego men and other non-violent techniques to galvanise communities, overthrow dictators or simply change the world".

5   Popovic, Srdja and Miller, Matthew, *Blueprint for Revolution: How to Use Rice Pudding, Lego Men, and Other Nonviolent Techniques to Galvanize Communities, Overthrow Dictators, or Simply Change the World*, Scribe, UK.

People talk about books that changed this life, well this was mine. It was one of the main sources of inspiration that encouraged me to start the Camerados movement in my bedroom in 2015. I don't mind that most people think that what we do is just comfy sofas and cups of tea, it kind of helps that people think that because that way they come in and sit down. Yet I'm hoping you're getting the idea that what's really going on in our public living rooms, if you dig a little deeper, is weirdly counter-cultural, and most systems, services and societies find it to be something of a revolutionary act. That's why Srdja's book gave me a huge jolt of hope and excitement.

I won't spoil the book for you, you really must read it, but there is story after story of people standing up to terrifying totalitarian regimes with fun, music and laughter. Srdja tells the story of Poland under communism, where people were so bored of the news, which just spewed the usual Moscow propaganda each night, that they took to putting their televisions on their window ledges at 6pm every night when the news broadcast began. You could look out of your apartment block window and see televisions outside windows as far as the eye could see. Then it got funnier. People started taking their televisions for a walk at news time. You could turn a corner and bump into someone else with their television in their wheelbarrow, and you'd both piss yourselves laughing. Yet you can't get arrested for pushing a wheelbarrow with a television set in it, so this act of defiance could go unpunished and people would feel a little hit of joy at their tiny triumph over fear and control. During the worst of President Assad's attacks on Aleppo, Srdja advised the local resistance to release thousands of ping pong balls into the streets with anti-Assad slogans written on each ball. The sight of the balls was funny enough, but funnier still was seeing Assad's forces racing after them trying to collect them up. And then there were the toys. When public protest became illegal in Belarus the locals put Lego men and other toys on the street holding little placards against the regime. When the news showed reports of police putting these toys into the backs of police vans, the people at home were holding their sides with laughter.

If you can find hope under tyranny surely we can find it where we live too? You don't need to live under a tyrant to feel helpless. Every day is the end of the world for somebody somewhere, even in a supposedly free, western society with dogs barking across sunny parks and people free to roam and sing and buy stuff. There will be somebody there who is crouched in the corner of their own mind hemmed in with their own problems and worries and deciding they can't make it through another day. And the hand that extends to them from our supposedly civilised world to offer help is often as cold and inhuman as the barrel of a gun in a war zone.

Melodramatic? Well, not if it drives you to the edge; and in many cases that is what happens. When you can't see a way forward, any unkindness feels like a fatal blow and in some ways being in a supposedly free, western society surrounded by others who seem happy, wealthy, carefree and loved is like salt in a wound. Being in crisis in our lucky world can feel like pressing a hungry face up against the window of a sumptuous restaurant. Yes, compared to Srdja's society we're lucky in so many respects, but not everybody is feeling it. Somewhere. Today.

I felt that if Srdja, and the people he helps, can bring change in the most hopeless places on the planet, surely we could make change in our street, in the inhuman systems I'd been working inside for twenty years, and even in our personal life. This guy brought hope and with it a lot of fun and laughter even in the darkest of places. So we decided to do the same.

So as well as bringing fairy lights, your grandma's couch and Connect Four into the world of life crises, we also wear big pants, we bring pianos to serious speaking gigs and more daft stuff which no doubt dents our credibility in some quarters and leads to a touch of ridicule.

We're not that concerned because our hunch is that it makes the room a little more human and somebody will be grateful for humanity peeking through the blinds of corporate seriousness. When people come up to us in the streets and ask why we're wearing giant underpants, we say "Cos life is pants sometimes" and we end up having some pretty big chats after that. It's quite different if we carried black and white photographs of people living in misery. I'm just not sure folk would stop to talk to us let alone open up.

I understand why the charity industry uses these sad images to raise money: quite simply, it works. Guilt and shame are powerful emotions and people reach inside their pockets to make the feeling go away. I saw this myself when, in a former life, in my early twenties I was a filmmaker. I made a film for Virgin Atlantic, the films on flights that ask you to leave your foreign change for charities in the little envelopes on your seat. We filmed in Moscow's orphanages, bloody awful places, but the kids I met were smart and inspiring, so I wrote an upbeat piano soundtrack while these beautiful resilient kids laughed and got their lives back thanks to a jaw-droppingly brilliant UK wheelchair charity called Motivation. The voiceover, by Jenny Agutter, told their positive, life-affirming story. "Nice try," said the editor putting it together for me in some editing suite in London's SoHo. "Fifty quid says next month's film kicks your arse." Next month's film had images of crying kids and a voiceover by a practically sobbing former royal princess Sarah Ferguson. I lost the bet, it kicked our arse, by about fifty grand.

But at what cost? I have to believe that the positive film attracted people to the cause much in the same way as the shame-inducing film repelled others to never want to see that again – just take my money!! When it comes to raising cash maybe this is the way forward, but if you want a relationship with a donor, or a passerby, then I'd always prefer to make them laugh and smile. People want to be around things that are fun. If it's fun, they'll join in. Of course, many people are recruited to cause shock and disgust. However, if we want to mobilise millions we need to make it joyful. A few diehard people will stick around your worthy project cos they believe in it, but you'll get the whole neighbourhood to take part if it makes them feel great.

Which is why whenever people ask us what the first step is when making a public living room we tell them to order pizza. Who doesn't love pizza? If you hold a meeting you'll attract local people who attend meetings. There is a certain kind of people who love a good local "consultation." Most people in your community would rather eat their own head. So make it worth their while. After pizza, start chatting and getting to know them and see where it goes.

It reminds me of the days my homeless hostel managers would say to me: "We tried your ideas Maff but nobody turned up." I'd ask them what they did next and they'd say, "Nothing, why bother, they're not interested." If you can't engage people maybe it's worth thinking about why they're not engaged? I remember one manager smugly throwing in my face that, "We tried to make things fun Maff like you said, we put on a canoe-ing trip and guess how many came?" I guessed the answer. "None. Not one person in the whole hostel. Waste of time." "Did you ask them if they liked canoe-ing?" I'd ask. Silence. Funnily enough, they hadn't. And in the hostel for homeless men mostly over 55 and predominantly drinkers, they probably would have discovered that dominos, darts or a trip to the dogs was more popular than a kayak on the river. If they'd asked.

When was the last time you had a really crappy day and thought to yourself, "I know what will cheer me up, I need to spend time with some government-funded agencies and get myself a support plan"? I'm suspecting never.

So what *do* your thoughts turn to? I reach for my piano. The music I love and more of it. And films, from Kubrick to Star Trek; a lamb roast or a fried breakfast in a British caff, which is most definitely my "happy place" surpassed only by the love of my life, the Great American Diner. Sports never did it for me, but for many of my friends it's what they turn to for joy and belonging, on a rainy, mud-sodden field or gravelly netball court with your friends chucking a ball about. Why do these things rarely make it onto a support plan for people going through a personal crisis? Well, sometimes they did.

The Salvation Army used to run a football cup competition every year between the hostels. Wherever I went in the country, residents were talking about it, staff too. It became the focus of everyone's year. These lads who had only recently been living on the streets or lost in some crack den were suddenly training like mad. They fundraised to buy their kit, they travelled in a minibus together to the game and they took half the hostel with them too for support. It was a great day out. One year we pushed the boat out and hired the stadium in Milton Keynes, but most years it was just in a few cages in Birmingham, a 5-a-side football complex on a housing estate. You'd have thought it was the World Cup though. The anticipation, the buzz in the air. When a lad went up to take a penalty you knew this was all he had in his life, that moment, that goal. The fairy tale moments came thick and fast as lads were held aloft by their teammates, lads who'd been told they were shit their whole life and believed it too. There was the camaraderie between players from wildly different backgrounds across the UK. The sportsmanly behaviour between people who society thought were not capable of such values. I could see people building relationships. I could see people committing to something and putting their heart into it because it mattered to them.

I couldn't measure a single housing or job outcome that day, yet I knew it was making more of a difference than a thousand days inside our hostels filling out support plans. There are ways to record outcomes when you're having fun though, you just have to be canny about it. The players in that tournament all knew how to tot up the points for their teams and figure out where they were in the standings. They had to fill in their entrance forms and were happy to do it if it meant they got a game. These were all skills, as was turning up on time and working as a team.

It's not radical to propose this kind of thing. Most services have some sort of fun activities going on. However, I'm never sure the system fully acknowledges that this should be the central work of the system, not a sideline, just a fun bit of nonsense. Engaging in fun helps people find themselves. Fun contains those two "meaning of life" ingredients – there's almost always friends, connection with others and some sense of purpose. The football game gave a huge injection of purpose into the lives of those homeless players and the connection with their team was huge too. Why is this belittled by systems? If you want your hard-hitting housing or job outcome then schools, colleges, rehabs, hostels, prisons surely have to focus on these kinds of activities. So many of the life improvement programmes we hurl at people come with horrific jargon-laden names, delivered in bland rooms with all the fun of an exam room. Rather than excite the neurons to new pathways, we revisit the trauma of failed times with brain-dulling, pressure-laden tests and programmes based on what a system wants, not the person who has to do all the "life-changing".

So if you want to inspire change – personal or societal – it's not a bad start to think about making people feel good. Populist politicians have certainly figured that one out. Srjda Popovic figured out you can powerfully erode the atmosphere of fear by being a bit silly. We can engage people more in a long-term mission of change if they get joy and nourishment from being involved, not just guilt and shame.

So why not start with one small act of rebellion in the most mundane setting of them all. A staff meeting. This is a little radical act you can all do probably, wherever you work. It comes from a camerado in Norwich called Sam. Sam's a bit of a legend, he's started so many public living rooms in different places that we've lost count (one beside a bike repair workshop; inside a board game night; one at a farmer's market; ... to mention just three). At the start of meetings in his local council where he worked, Sam would dread the inevitable "round of introductions". So instead of saying his name and his job title – as everybody does – he would say

"Hi I'm Sam and my favourite biscuit is a Hob Nob".

People would stare. Embarrassing silence would follow. But only for a second cos soon people would smile or giggle and then something remarkable would happen. The next person would say their name and then pause and say " ... my favourite biscuit is a Jammy Dodger actually". Cue laughter around the table. It became infectious. More introductions would include biscuit confessions until everyone around the whole table had stated their strong and passionate biscuit affiliations. I know it's daft and it's a very tiny thing to do but something amazing does come from it. The meeting will be much more effective, people will see each other as humans not job titles and get to a much deeper level of human understanding and it will happen much quicker too. Something as small as that can unlock the human.. So put down the bombs you intended to drop in that meeting and reach for your big pants, your biscuit confessions, your own brand of silly. You may find you achieve a lot more in the process!

BELFAST

A big bear of a man, white, rugged, in his sixties, angry looking, strode purposefully over to a group of six or seven Deliveroo cyclists, all of whom were from Eritrea, who were sitting in our public living room for orders to come in from the massive McDonald's on the other side of the road. He pointed at the Connect Four on the table and raised his eyebrows. They accepted the challenge, the big guy knelt down on our rug, one of the Eritreans did the same opposite him and his friends all gathered round. They all threw banter at him in a language we didn't recognise, though we discovered later that there are nine official languages in Eritrea. The big guy took on all of them, placing his Connect Four tokens in the slots with flourish. Some games he won, some he lost and each time whoops would go up, laughter resounded and a full twenty minutes was spent without any need for a common language. At the end of his lunch-hour, the big bear guy high-fived them all and waved in the air as his back walked down the street and a guard of honour of Deliveroo cyclists applauded him into the distance.

Our Eritrean friends stayed with us all day that time in Belfast. At first they had eyed us suspiciously when we were setting up and they sat on municipal benches and perched on litter bins nearby. They edged closer, and sat on the kerb closer to us for the next hour. Then eventually two of them ventured onto two armchairs and played Connect Four. They didn't know the rules so we showed them then left them to it. Before long the whole gang sat with us.

Later, as the day ended, I was struggling with the furniture across the road to the van when our Connect Four players all jumped up and took care of the whole operation for me, without being asked. A line of Deliveroo drivers carrying sofas, armchairs, rugs and tables across Donegal Street and into my van, which was sat with the hazard lights on outside McDonald's. Suddenly a local man with a small yappy-type dog came rushing out of the door and ran at them: "Everyone in McDonald's says you're stealing that furniture!" He didn't see me inside the back of the van. I poked my head around the van door and informed him that they were actually being exceptionally helpful to me. The fella looked confused, didn't issue an apology and walked back inside McDonald's. I quickly googled the Eritrean for "Sorry" and "Thank you" but all the guys just smiled at me and threw their hands up in the air. They get it a lot.

But mostly people came together. A local musician with a guitar joined us and busked in the public living room and her beautiful, pure Irish-lilting voice bounced off the grand stone buildings all around us, a natural reverb lending an otherworldly echo to her songs. It didn't last long though, as suddenly a booming sound erupted and could be heard everywhere: "YOU ARE GOING TO HELL!" said a voice. People around me shuddered and their eyes darted between the buildings, the echo making it hard to see where this headless, booming was coming from. "YOU HAVE BEEN NOTICED." Was this some disapproving giant? A mythical beast with a distaste for my soft furnishings and pavement shenanigans? I had been moved on and ejected from the pavements many times by security or police but this was a new one. "YOU FACE A LIFE OF FIRE AND DAMNATION." Crikey! It was getting a little frightening now. Then I turned around and saw a little black speaker by a bus stop outside a Costa Coffee with a black lead extending from it, winding past a litter bin and into a microphone gripped by hands belonging to a small man in a beige jacket and jeans with a comb-over haircut. " ... IF YOU TURN YOUR BACK ON JESUS."

This was Pete, originally from Omagh, and he belonged to an evangelical church that saves souls outside Costa on Donegal Street, Mondays and Wednesdays usually between 10 and 12 o'clock. This is what he told us when we asked if it might be possible for him to not compete with our friend's busking and move his very loud speaker to a different spot. He was a nice enough fella, but wasn't up for moving. We sensed the Holy Spirit had ordained it that this was the absolute best place in the city centre to save folk from hellfire and damnation. Hard to argue with that. Our valiant busker carried on and for the next half hour our ears had to endure beautiful songs by Christy Moore remixed with a layer of shouty Ezekiel and Isaiah verses rapped by a middle-aged man from County Tyrone.

Eventually, the woman who set up the regular Camerados public living room in the city turned up. She's called Dawn and runs a remarkable centre for homeless families called Thorndale, which is the epitome of caring, empathetic, human services, but faced with Pete the evangelist, well Dawn was having none of it. One of the nicest, most smiley, friendliest people you could meet, when Dawn turns, she turns. She deploys her Belfast accent like she's spreading butter with a machete and all we saw from the other side of the street was Pete having an on-the-spot conversion. We don't know what was said, but he must have seen the light and realised souls could be saved outside other budget sports fashion outlets in the city that day.

With the busker's haunting refrains restored, minus accompaniment, came a horde of strangers to watch, sit, play games and also dance. A man, who looked like he was sleeping on the streets, put his sleeping bag down and broke into a very expressive set of dance moves. He was truly letting go. Some passing kids whooped and, though they were probably taking the piss, the guy took it as encouragement and waved back at them – he was in the zone and didn't care. Alongside him danced a visiting couple from Melbourne sporting fleeces and sensible jeans. The homeless man danced with them and I can't tell you how hard it is for me to resist saying "They were different worlds united by one language, the joy of dancing" because then I'd have to eat my own head. But there I said it. These three people owned the dance floor or pavement opposite McDonald's as it was – much to the amusement of a crowd that had gathered to observe and cheer or jeer them on. The Melbourne couple told me later that they'd sold their house in Australia and just hit the road to see the world, and that they'd figure out where to live when they got back at some point. Their business had become too stressful, and when one of them had a serious health scare they felt there was more to life and sold up. "People are more important than things," they said. "Which is why we've stayed in Belfast as long as we have, the people here are so generous and lovely."

This had been my observation too. I must confess it's hard to understand how these people spent so long blowing each other up when their hospitality is as good as it is. How can this be a place known for division and hate when I found them to be the most proactively generous and welcoming people I have met in the UK. I saw examples of this time and time again and could never quite reconcile it with the street murals and graffiti aimed at inciting sectarian violence.

I found this up the road in Lisburn too. I'd visited a food bank there because they'd tagged a public living room onto it so that people could get a bit of companionship whilst picking up their free pasta and tins of food. Like Karen had found in Lochgilphead, it helped reduce the stigma. "I thought I'd just pop in for a cuppa to say hello and look out for ya Keith"; "Would you help us out Mary and take some of this bread with you? We can't get rid of it"; "Oh well sure, since I'm here I might as well, thanks now".

The poverty was striking. The food bank/public living room was through a door in a car park, and, the day before I visited, a woman couldn't wait until getting to her car to leave before eating, so she sat on the tarmac of the car park and ate the ready meal there and then. She had so little that she had been feeding her kids instead of herself for so many days that she was due to faint, so she ripped off the lid and scooped a Carbonara into her mouth, not caring who saw her. This story was told to me by the woman – and force of nature – who volunteered at the food bank and ran countless other free drop-ins for folk in the area. A small bundle, freckly, long hair with bright eyes and a beautiful smile, Tracey had been the general manager of a very big supermarket, one of the big chains. Despite her many years of much-admired service, their HR dept dispatched her from her job for reasons unknown and did so with such inhuman language that the story of this trauma is never far from Tracey's opening conversation with strangers. Her health isn't great and she struggles to walk. Yet despite this, she offers me a lift into Belfast and a tour of the sights. She can't possibly afford the petrol and the effort must be painful for her, yet she won't hear a "No" from me. Generosity isn't just kindness, it's kindness in the face of adversity, kindness from people without much to feel kind about.

Meanwhile back on the pavement in Belfast a lad in a Martian mask fell asleep on the sofa with us, mask still on. Beside him a black woman with a beautiful bright green jacket and yellow running shoes sits down and asks me what this is all about. "It's a public living room," I say. She's in her sixties, her fiery eyes scan the furniture, the corners of her mouth turn up into a disapproving smirk and she says, in a looping, lyrical, bouncing American accent, "And I suppose that explanation helps me how exactly?" "Well what do you think it means," I continue, unhelpfully. The conversation unfurls until she puts the concept of a living room with the concept of something public and then we expand into why this might be useful.

She is from Detroit originally, but spent most of her life further south as she worked as the head librarian in a top Ivy League University. She's starting her retirement by seeing the world. I ask how Belfast made it onto her list and she looks me dead in the eye and says, "I feel like these people understand me cos we had tanks on the streets of Detroit too."

She tells me that she grew up in the place where people live when they get thrown out of the projects. It was poorer than poor. She told me how she would look on wryly when colleagues at her University would talk about poverty and social justice as if they had any clue what it felt like or how they were making her feel by talking about it. When she was nine years old she remembers screaming in their apartment and her mother opening the door and telling her she had to run now. She remembers looking back up the stairwell at her mum closing the door and there being more screaming. Next thing she remembers she's in a burger joint called White Castle across the street and everyone is staring at her. A large, white woman with flowing blonde hair appears behind her, takes off her big green coat, one of those duvet-like winter jackets, and puts it around her whole body and legs and only then does she realise that she had been sitting in White Castle in only her panties. The waitresses and the customers all looked after her that night, fed her and waited for her mom. She left Detroit that night and didn't see her Daddy again.

"WHERE DO WE STAND ON BLOWJOBS?"

The idea that if you want to be more human, a little trust helps.

It's 4am on Christmas Eve in a homeless shelter in East London and a woman is shouting my name hysterically somewhere off in the distance.

The scene is a classic Dickensian set up. Rows of wooden camp beds laid out in a large brick warehouse with people tacking their way through labyrinths of sprawled out sleeping bodies and discarded styrofoam boxes of food. Some people sit in groupings of plastic chairs holding cans and chatting, some wander up to a kitchen hatch for a cup of tea. A transistor radio plays crappy supermarket Christmas songs and the air stinks of wet dog and cigarettes.

This is 2002, and when I first filled out the form to volunteer for the charity Crisis (some years prior to this) I put "Any shift, Any shelter" on the form, only for my letter to come back saying I had been assigned "Night shift, Drinkers shelter". The only shelter where people were allowed to drink, and a shift from 10 at night til 8am the following morning. I remember gulping. Yet now I loved this place more than you can imagine. It felt like the rest of the world did bullshit and tinsel and we were in the proverbial stable, only instead of a donkey and the holy family there was Alan with a bottle of Diamond White telling stories about his time in the SAS, and Sandra a Whitechapel sex worker bumming fags off him and showing us her tattoo of Alec Baldwin.

The woman's shouting was coming closer. The shift leader, which I had become, had a makeshift office made out of MDF and plasterboard and I was taking a moment's rest in my chair whilst chatting to George and Rick, two assistant shift leaders wearing heavy coats and dirty jeans who were boiling a kettle and rolling tobacco. The door was flung open with such gusto it almost fell apart. The woman stood there, she was in her fifties wearing a wax jacket and cashmere jumper which made her look like she was off to a grouse shoot, not volunteering at a homeless shelter. She glared at us with a face of horror. We all looked up with expressions that said: "What's up?"

She couldn't breathe from her exertion but just signalled for us to follow her in the direction of the toilet block. We raced after her. The night before we had to eject a gang of particularly bolshy crack dealers who had viewed our shelter as a very convenient and ready-made marketplace and I was not in a hurry to repeat the experience. So, as I followed grouse-shoot lady, I was expecting more of the same and trying to calm my nerves.

We arrived at the toilets. It was a Portacabin on wheels, the kind you see at festivals, where each cubicle had a gap of about a foot at the base of the door. When we entered she told me to look underneath the third cubicle. I looked and saw the feet and legs of someone seated and the feet and legs of someone kneeling in front and facing them. I turned back to the volunteer. With horror in her eyes she addressed me with disgust in her voice and said, "Where do we stand on blow jobs?".

George, Rick and I stood in silence and took a beat to look at each other. Then I said to her, "I think we're in favour of them."

It's moments like this which reveal so much about how we see each other. Why did that woman think people who are homeless shouldn't be having sex? Are they a different species? Or maybe she thought of them as children in our care, to be chided for filthy behaviour? Why should she have an opinion on it at all?

It's back to the stuff we discussed in the Crap Lives Matter chapter. Perhaps like so many places that I worked, she wanted those people receiving her charity to be supplicatory and saintly, the deserving poor who were, primarily, grateful to her. I know I'm being hard on this very well-intentioned woman but actually it was an incident that just threw into sharp relief how we honestly view people who we perceive worse off than ourselves. "Where do we stand on blowjobs?" wasn't the question here, what we heard was: "How dare these people think they're just like us!"

When I started Camerados I hoped it was a way to take off the weird goggles society has put on us and remind us to see each other and be more human. What I'd like to touch on here, which I didn't in the Crap Lives Matter chapter, is the issue of trust. I said earlier we can't do anything without confidence. A powerful way to give people confidence is to trust them. We don't need to babysit them, guard their behaviour all of the time, certainly not in the toilets.

When we started Camerados we tried a different model from public living rooms to help people find friends and purpose. It was an idea with a horrible clunky name: Rapid Micro-Business Programme. The gist was that we took a bunch of people with tough lives and we worked with them to start their own business in four weeks. The idea was that pulling together to meet the challenge and start trading and earning their own money would galvanise them and bring them together around this big sense of self worth and purpose. We did this in Blackpool, Lincoln, Sheffield and Oxford, starting a smoothie making business (where punters pedalled a bike that powered a food processor!); an artisan wood carving business; and a tea dance business (where old people got out the house and had a dance, so tackling isolation as an extra boost!).

Our first, though, was in Blackpool and we were working with a group of 10 folk, all of whom were addicts of either alcohol, crack, heroin or new psychotic substances. The business they decided to start was a Christmas wrapping service. So we found ourselves, the week before Christmas outside Debenhams, dressed as Christmas elves and taking people's expensive gifts and wrapping them for two quid a pop. There was a big buzz and customers flocked to us. To be fair, we had neglected a fairly important part of the business plan, which we discovered on Day One: none of us were any good at wrapping presents. However, we soon developed a company slogan "Put a fucking bow on it", which was usually accompanied by much wheezing laughter and mirth under our pointy ear hats. Two things about trust emerged which blew my mind. One happened when we ran out of wrapping paper. I handed a fellow elf and Camerado my wallet, and

143

told him to go get some more. The young lad I handed it to just froze for a second or two, and glared at me. We held my wallet between us for a few seconds until he nodded and left. At the end of business that day he told me that had been quite a moment for him. Nobody had ever trusted him like that for a long while. After that he was quite a different worker, always showed up and worked harder than the rest. If he'd stolen my wallet I would have lost fifty quid in cash and had to cancel all my cards. Hardly comparable to the priceless appreciation of trust he felt, which had such a great effect on him.

The second story is less happy. One weekend we decided to leave them to run the stall themselves. Yes we gulped, yes we were nervous but how else were they gonna run their own business if we were always hanging around? After the weekend's trading we got a phone call from the agency who were working with each of them, their support workers. They wanted a word. We arrived at the agency's office to find a lot of smirking people shaking their heads at us. "You can't trust them, you know. You've been very naive," they said. They went on to tell us that the tin that contained all the money was short, some money had been taken, thirty pounds was gone, "stolen" they said. We asked how much money was in the tin. "About £400," they told us. We laughed. "Have you met a crack addict?" I asked. The crack addicts I was used to working with wouldn't leave £400 behind, they'd have taken it all *and* flogged the tin as well. This was a major success, by any measure. When we met with the Elves it turned out there was an explanation for the missing thirty pounds too. It was called lunch. And they had kept the receipt.

Trust is a fantastic way of showing people they are on the level with you. That I'm not better than you. This is why in Camerados we believe in practising mutuality more than charity. Revisiting that theme of Social Darwinism, it's a shame that the philosophers and politicians of the day had not read another thinker of the time: Pyotr Kropotkin.

Kropotkin spoke of the virtues of mutuality and associational life. He pointed out that this was a natural inclination in humans and had emerged at various points of human history. He pointed out that it was also common in the natural world. Whereas Darwin filled our heads with the cut-throat world of natural selection, Kropotkin pointed out that birds would co-operate on the bird table, waiting for others to feed first; wolves hunted in packs; chimpanzees worked as a family. This isn't to paint a utopian picture of the often fierce and dangerous natural world, but it does show that there is an acknowledgement, too, of the power of working together and supporting the weaker among us. It breeds belonging and a feeling of being valued and trusted. It also gets things done! We sometimes call it "The Sugar Question".

The Sugar Question

Once in a public living room a man walked over to the table where teas and coffees were available and announced to the room, "You've run out of sugar." Somebody shouted back: "You'd better get some sugar then." The man paused, looked quizzical and walked out. "You've lost him," someone else said watching him leave. However, ten minutes later, the man returned holding a Sainsbury's bag and he told the room, "We've got sugar" and everyone cheered.

The first assumption for many of us is that sugar will be provided. We are entitled to sugar, that's the usual transaction. When it's pointed out to people, however, they are very often all too happy to be trusted with the job of figuring things out. If a service has all the answers then where is the room for other people's agency? Where's the room for them to feel trusted?

I'm going to conclude this chapter by talking about an area where trust is so lacking that things can get scary and dangerous. The world of Safeguarding. This is a word that is used a lot in services in the UK and it has become a little like shouting "fire" in a crowded room. When done badly, all things go into a state of panic, people's IQs often plummet and steel gates come down. I'm not saying that it isn't extremely important to safeguard the welfare of adults and children, of course it is. We must be aware of the risks and manage them well. The only problem is that a lot of people with a half-knowledge of true safeguarding risk use it as a reason to not do good things.

The main "good thing" is to trust people. We throw out the word "Safeguarding" and everyone immediately accepts why some great project can't go ahead. The immediate assumption is that some terrifying crime would occur so it's best not proceed. We get it a lot with public living rooms.

People being left to run a space themselves, left to talk about all sorts of things, probably including the tough times in their life ... this is too risky. "They may disclose something and we would need to throw a containment plan around," one staff member of a Further Education college told us once. We asked them if they knew about every conversation that went on between students in Costa Coffee? And if Costa had a safeguarding policy and a containment plan? People talk in parks and the park rangers don't rush over and stop it if it's too heavy.

Hopefully the fact that students feel relaxed and comfortable enough to talk about big stuff in a public living room is better than them hiding it and keeping it to themselves. Our principles mean that nobody has the responsibility to fix things and take responsibility for what they hear. A former Chief Social Worker of England, Fran Leddra, wrote recently that Camerados public living rooms are in themselves a great safeguarding approach. When people can be seen, when they are talking about issues, this reduces risk of harm. When problems are hidden behind doors, when we can't see people and whether they are going downhill, this is when we worry. Better to get them on a sofa, with a cuppa, looking out for each other and seeing each other as human ... not a safeguarding risk.

LEICESTER

A father sat on one of our sofas, in the rain, a light drizzle, his arm tightly around his daughter. He was white English, she was Indian, perhaps in her thirties and with a learning disability, and the pair were resting their feet before an art group. "We go to lots of groups," the father said. "We know all the people there now. We also have an allotment. It's good to keep busy and be around people." They didn't chat much but just sat with us. I was surprised they stayed, as ever since we arrived in the epicentre of Leicester, around the clock tower, our sofas had been colonised by a group rough sleepers, one of whom was so tired for another restless night on the pavement he slept soundly beside it, outstretched on the bean bag sofa. They were peaceful but the father looked like a slightly frightened nervous guy. Yet this community was not a problem for him. He and his daughter were part of *our* little group that morning, no allotment or arts but company at least.

Some loud music came from behind us. Trombones, trumpets, drums. It seemed to be coming towards us. Suddenly, a wall of people appeared all marching down the streets. A protest. NHS staff, banners aloft, chants above the music, everyone looking quite jolly despite the subject matter. The homeless guy sleeping on the sofa woke up and along with his pals all cheered and held their fists aloft in solidarity. Some of the protesters waved back and made the same gesture.

Derek, flat cap, very neat, late sixties, stands very still just watching us in the street. He's not waiting for a bus, he doesn't seem to be waiting for anyone. It becomes a bit unnerving after a while so I wander over to say Hi. There's no "hello" in return, he just launches straight into something I sort of felt he'd been preparing. "This city was ruined once all these bloody spear carriers moved into the city. I suppose you're a charity worker are you?" Gotta say, that caught me off guard right there and then. So I didn't do my usual thing of trying to engage with a racist and I just said "Nope" and wandered back to my sofa. I do genuinely believe in engaging with folk with these views, but I also stand by the rule that allows you not to have to do it if you don't want to that day! Sometimes you know you haven't got the right energy for it, and being with the young Indian girl with learning difficulties and watching the devotion and love from her father I just didn't entirely trust myself not to be horrible to Derek, which wouldn't have helped anyone. So I removed myself.

We moved location and went into a park but the rain didn't stop so we put up our gazebo. As I always found with the gazebo, passersby assumed we were selling TV subscriptions or membership to the Automobile Association so didn't approach the furniture let alone sit down with us. All except Keto.

Keto was from Somalia and fled the war. He was now studying at De Montfort University. He sat with us for ages, not always talking and often reading the *Viz* magazine we had with us. I regretted buying *Viz*, the ribald humour hardly being everyone's taste, but then I saw Keto chuckling to himself, so I was relieved.

"I want to go home one day," he said. "I have family and friends which means I have direction, I know my way, there is hopefulness. Here I don't know anybody. I play pool sometimes with people but that's it."

Public living rooms
from around the world

Rochdale

THE 3RD WAY TO DEAL WITH "DIFFICULT" BEHAVIOUR

The idea that there is another way to handle hostile situations and it can be more effective and inclusive

Society tends to have two responses to difficult behaviour.

Often the solution is to ban people, exclude them from the project. Unfortunately that often just creates an enemy and you find your front windows smashed in over the weekend. You've certainly got someone wandering the streets holding a grudge and letting that distrust of their fellow man grow until they take it out on someone else.

The other approach is to let people stay, despite their behaviour, on account that they don't have the faculties to understand what is wrong and we need to be endlessly patient. Unfortunately that often results in patronising the person and, worse, means your project will be empty soon because nobody else feels safe there. If this is the kind of place that isn't going to deal with the fella throwing chairs across the room then who is going to feel safe and stick around.

However, there is a third option. As usual, it features a cup of tea and a biscuit accompanied by a fairly unwavering message.

If you deliver a straight message to someone, treating them like a fellow adult, face to face, looking people in the eye with a cuppa that says I don't hate you ... then they will listen more and feel respected. The message is still: "This behaviour is not OK and will not be tolerated." The message is still to ask them to leave too, although with an important addition: "Come back tomorrow or whenever you can respect others."

The reaction is very different from the enemy caving in your windows or the person who thinks they got away with it and then continues to take the piss.

They may – in the moment – continue to swear and rail against you and even storm off; and this has happened to me many times. However, what happens next is interesting. Without fail, they return the next day and don't want to speak to anyone else but you. And they shake your hand and apologise. Sometimes I've even had flowers, and chocolates!

I reckon that the thought process they've gone through while they've been away is that they were spoken to like an equal and a person of value. They were levelled with. And of course beneath their bluff and bluster on some level they know that their behaviour wasn't OK. That has, however, to some extent been dealt with and there's a way back – rather than it festering and eroding their feelings about themselves. The overriding feeling is that the behaviour was bad but not the person. If someone is thrown out without discussion, it feels more personal. If they've been allowed to stay despite unacceptable behaviour then there's still a part of themselves that has not been challenged and possibly feels bad about themselves too, maybe not, but it's possible.

Amazing really that just levelling with people softly can result in such a transformative effect. The best policemen have learnt this and so have teachers and all sorts of people in public-facing jobs. Yet many organisations force their employees to jettison this simple human instinct in favour of exclusion policies. In the charity world, there are also saviours who go the other way and continue to accept rising and rising levels of danger because they think it's the "kindest" thing to do. I would venture that the kindest act is to be honest and straight with people who have wronged you, directly to them not to anyone else.

Obviously this isn't for everyone. It can be scary. I was scared when doing it with Amadi (a man I meet in the next chapter) and I felt sad afterwards. However, I could also have left and come back later. That is always a choice open to you too. We don't have to deal with things where we feel unsafe; we can remove ourselves too. We call them "public living rooms" so do what you might do in public. The laws of the land still stand. Call the police if you want to, leave if you want to.

There was a public living room recently that struggled with a man who kept using racist language and it upset people and rightly required challenging. The woman who called up our team didn't feel comfortable being the one to level with him. So we suggested they find other people who did and for more than one to sit down with him over a cuppa and talk to him about it. They offered him the chance to come back another day when he could respect how they felt and see that it upset people. Nothing bad happened and he left. He hasn't come back since, but they are hopeful he might one day. There's always an open door but each and every time we can be straight about things and ask folk to leave.

A woman in New York who worked with us in the early days said to us: "Maff, New Yorkers are already natural Camerados. We help a brother out, but we don't take no shit." That pretty much nails it.

BURNLEY

Gustav sat down as soon as the legs of the sofa hit the pavement. He told me he was a "retired punk rocker". He looked the part with pink hair, a straw hat and a face sculptured by decades of mighty mayhem. He told me stories of his tours, how music brought people together regardless of language and politics. I was gripped when he recalled how he played as the Berlin Wall came down, right beside the wall, literally as it was being hacked and pulled down.

Gustav now has a phone from his key worker that he doesn't know how to use. The worker didn't tell him so it's just locked and useless – he shows it to me. "Bit Kafka-esque!" he says, "somewhat nihilistic of the system don't you think! I kinda love it. Reminds me I'm right to be an anarchist!" He pockets his pointless phone and lets the sun warm his face. Others in the group who know him tell me Gustav is well known locally for wandering the streets of Burnley talking to everyone. He told me, "Everyone is lovely back to me. We're nothing without community." He adds, "And music!"

At various points of the day a succession of kids on study leave bring their "MaccyDs" into the public living room and eat them, leaving most of the detritus of their meal behind. Note to self: don't pop up on a pavement too near a McDonald's and provide them with an additional seating area.

"Oh man this is brain space. This is what I don't have."

This was said by a tall, handsome west African man called Amadi. He told me that his anxieties were loud inside his head and his flat was noisy and unsafe.

Outside in the world too he felt on edge always. It turns out he had a very real reason to feel this way. He showed me scars from knife attacks – on his arms and his head. All these attacks were racially motivated, he told me. Amadi had the air of an intellectual, he wanted me to know about his various degrees in Nigeria and how he hadn't wanted to come here but he had to – he didn't explicitly say he fled Nigeria but he inferred as much. He had lost everything including how people saw him, a learned fellow. He then told me a story that began in such an anodyne ordinary fashion and spiralled in a way that is so shocking it reveals both how things can get out of hand so quickly and easily with people who are judged and experience prejudice, and also how injustice can be present in the most average, everyday life. You probably think that's a dramatic assessment. Listen to Amadi. This story is also difficult for me to tell because, though nothing compared to Amadi's experience, it was the only time, ever, in a public living room that I was scared. I'm sure it will shake some of your confidence in the whole idea of these spaces but it's important to tell the tough stories too. The word is "public" which means you're gonna meet everyone and anyone and of course anything can happen. Most of all I want you to hear this man's story because he deserves to be heard.

He told me that his building society had incorrectly charged his account and this had put him in a precarious financial position, so much so that he lost sleep. He had been on the website with little success and then telephoned them endlessly until he finally got through to someone who told him he had to go into a branch and speak to someone in person. He duly spent the bus fare with what little money he had left and headed into town to the branch. When he got there they said they couldn't help him in the branch and he'd have to do it all online. He was naturally upset about this but when he raised his voice they reacted disproportionately strongly with him. He told me that a tall black man being upset has a different reaction around these parts. He was just expressing his frustration; he wasn't causing damage or abusing anyone verbally yet before he knew it a team of armoured police men came through the door. Naturally he was alarmed and started shouting at them too, at which point he was struck by one of the policemen and it broke his wrist – he showed me the damage.

As Amadi relayed these events I could see he was reliving the trauma. He became animated and started directing his anger towards me. This is the lasting corrosive damage that inhuman behaviour, unkindness, violence and, in this case, most likely blatant racism does to people. He was a mess in front of me and now he was raising his voice and making everyone in the public living room feel uncomfortable. I asked him to lower his voice because he was scaring people. He didn't, he said I was just like the police. I asked him if he knew a good coffee shop nearby? The temperature dropped and he said that he did. I asked him if he could take me there as I needed a coffee. He agreed and we exited the public living room, leaving folks to relax again and we went into a local café on the corner. Behind the counter was a stocky Iranian man in his fifties with a white beard and a kind smile. Amadi was suddenly venting his anger, again, to nobody in particular, just a random explosion of expletives and he was bobbing on his feet agitatedly. I threw the owner a look that said "sorry about this" and as he handed us our coffees he said a surprising but wonderful thing "This is a good man, a gentle man," signalling towards Amadi. Amadi's community had his back.

When we returned to the sofas on our patch of wasteland, Amadi returned to calm and thanked me. Nobody listened and he needed a place to be accepted and listened to, he said. Just when I was feeling pretty good about what we were doing, he changed again in an instant, some fragment of memory, of the trauma, leaping again into his mind and he began prodding his finger at me. He started saying he wanted to hurt and harm those police officers, next time he'd stab them and punch them and ... on it went. I handed him a biscuit I'd got from the café, swigged my last bit of tea then asked him very politely to leave and come back later. He called me all sorts of names, flinging his arms about and strode off swearing and cursing at the world.

We've never had a violent incident in a public living room in the nine years communities have been running, including ones open 24 hours a day beside Accident & Emergency wards in hospitals. However, I was scared in this instant. I'm still shaken up by it when I think of it. I felt so horrible for Amadi, what he had been through was unconscionable, but I was anxious for myself too. We have a Camerados principle of "It's OK to disagree respectfully" so that people feel they have permission to ask someone to leave or if they are not confident to do so, to leave themselves. Observe "the law of two feet" and just leave. These are public spaces; we all meet situations we don't want to be in anymore and just leave. There's no expectation to fix anyone so that compulsion is not present either. Is it a cop out? I don't think so. I was shaken up and feeling guilty about asking Amadi to leave when he was going through something so terrible, but then he was continuing a cycle of violence and it's perfectly fine to say you're not OK with it, because that then provides a boundary for him too. He needed to exit that situation as well.

Obviously I'm vexed to this day about this situation and what is best for Amadi? He began by saying he needed space to rest his thoughts and be accepted, but then ended up in a bad place. Should I be trained in dealing with trauma? Well, there are very good places for that and setting up members of the public to only connect in our spaces if they are "trained" just undermines the whole "public", non-service, non-professional aspect of it that people so value and desperately crave. People want to have a bit of company with people who are not trained to be with them. I have to hope that on some days Amadi would get a lot from it and others he wouldn't, because that happens anywhere. It did remind me that people walk our streets carrying unspeakably tough stories inside them and it's quite remarkable that when these collide with other people and their stories we still somehow manage to have a vaguely functioning world. Well, until we don't, and we wage war and commit injustices to one another. If you're reading this and can help me think through how I could have handled the situation with Amadi better please do let me know.

My sadness that day pales into pointless consideration compared with Amadi's titanic struggles but, for what it's worth, I was glad to have a Camerado with me that day, a colleague who came in the van with me (illustrator of this book, Victoria). As I'm writing this, you can probably hear I'm still struggling with it. Yet Victoria reminded me that this thing we do is not meant to be an elixir for all ills, it's just a tiny bit of vital humanity in someone's day. When he reflects back on *his* day perhaps this thought will permeate Amadi's sadness, that somebody listened and there was humanity somewhere. Perhaps not. After all, this isn't about fixing things; however, there's an increased chance of that happening after we connected.

Public living rooms
from around the world
Taupo
New Zealand

TALKING BOLLOCKS

The idea that how we speak to people is awful.

Even the positive stuff.

It's Wednesday evening and I'm at a board meeting. I'm the fairly new Chief Executive of a national charity working in homelessness, domestic violence, criminal justice and community development, and I have a great board of trustees sat around me. We are joined by someone new this evening, a man in his thirties with a short shaved haircut, a lived-in face and a white Reebok branded sweatshirt. He uses one of our services in Liverpool for "high risk and prolific ex-offenders". He has travelled down with a key worker to attend the board meeting at my request. This is what is called "service user involvement" and somewhere I'm getting a big tick in an inclusivity box for asking him to join the board meeting where we are deciding the new brand for our charity.

I feel strongly about the language we use in the social justice world and how it obfuscates the issues affecting people's lives (love the fact I just made that point and used the word "obfuscate" without self awareness or irony) so I went on one of my rants in front of the board about it. I was probably slightly grandstanding and showing off my credentials as a young, thrusting, radical leader. I think the point I was trying to make is let's not hide behind words, let's just say it like it is and talk about how we work with people who are "poor". Let's just talk about "poverty" and use the word "poor". It cuts through all the nonsense and says it like it is.

The man from Liverpool, who had a name actually and it was Derek, suddenly said something but nobody could hear it. I asked him to repeat it.

He leant forward and rather shyly said to everyone: "I don't want my kids hearing that. I don't want them knowing their old man is living in a place that helps the poor."

Some of you are reading the coarse language in this chapter title – indeed the whole book – and tutting under your breath aren't you? Well, I'm glad you had that reaction. Language can give us that – extraordinary isn't it?! Words on a page or words from someone's mouth have an almost physical reaction and sensation in our body. And in this case presumably the reaction was a negative one; perhaps you were a bit disappointed in me for trying to be shocking and edgy when it really wasn't needed. So does that mean that you've got an opinion of me now? Based on one word I used? So what opinion do you think people have when they are going through the worst day of their life, some terrible personal crisis perhaps, and they turn up to get help somewhere and the first words they read or hear are "mental health drop in centre" or "substance misuse clinic" or they are presented with a "Needs and Risk Assessment" (which presumably is talking about everything that is wrong with you and all the risks that you pose). Do we think they will have a reaction to that on some level and perhaps form an opinion of those who use this odd language? What would that reaction and opinion be? I'm assuming it's "Get the hell out of here and away from these people".

The argument goes that this is just a convenient label and not to overthink it because what else are you going to call these issues. I know I've spent many years in different charities arguing over whether we could find a new name for "service users" as the term is rubbish, and we never found a good replacement because they all come loaded with something and "service user" was the least offensive and most descriptive. This is why we use Camerado.

Yet if language makes you feel something, how do you feel when someone refers you to a class in "basic life skills"? Am I the only one who hears that and thinks, "Wow I must be totally useless at life if you're sending me there."

In the same way that I make the case in this book that our notions of charity are still stuck in the parent/child dynamic from the 19th century or earlier, I am also making the same case for the language we use. It isn't that much more advanced than the old "homes for the disturbed" or "hospitals for the insane" that existed 100 years ago. We classify and create people as an "other" and we really make them feel spectacularly messed up about themselves in the process.

Deficit language is quicker and simpler and so the system loves it. Always much easier to talk about what people lack than what they have to offer. When Lord Scarman was asked by Margaret Thatcher to lead an enquiry into the Brixton Riots the language at the time was all about "broken homes", "disadvantaged youths" and so on. What Scarman found, and to his credit spoke about, was a community brimming with talents and enviable sense of community and belonging. Yet "Brixton" is burnt into the social history of Britain as a place of firebombs and crime. This left a lot of people who could have invested in the area thinking that too and worse it left its own residents believing it too. But it wasn't true, despite the problems and the subsequent unrest this was a place with a lot going for it.

So at this point you're thinking I'm going to want to flip the narrative and ask you to use aspirational, asset-based language. Well, just to be difficult I'm here to tell you that there's a problem with that too!

The positive "aspirational" language can be almost worse than the deficit words, because they are somehow more dishonest and manipulative. Charities have, in great numbers, rebranded themselves with new names, new funky business cards and eye-catching logos – I myself have been guilty of this.

There are lots of charities with names and logos that suggest we're reaching for the stars with taglines that talk about "change" and "transformation". When you're on the bones of your arse and wondering whether your kids will starve this week or maybe you might lose them entirely, these words have a rather hollow and wicked sound to them at times. The thing is that these are not words that any vaguely socially aware person would use in normal conversation, yet we emblazon them on our mastheads. In all my life, I never welcomed a homeless person into one of my hostels with the words:

"Hi Trevor, do you fancy unlocking your potential today?"

Trevor would no doubt tell me exactly where to stick my unlocked potential and I wouldn't blame him.

Alan was a wiry sort of bloke, six foot tall in his sixties and a bit like a skinny Michael Caine but without the specs, wearing mostly denim. He had been in the Army, a Guards regiment, for 20 years serving overseas including The Falklands War. When he came out he was a shop steward in a factory. Had a wife and four kids but lost them, and the job, for reasons I never really got to the bottom of but I'm pretty sure it was his childhood relationships and the heavy drinking he did to block it out. He finally stopped kipping on the streets one Christmas because the cold was gonna kill him. From one of our shelters he made it into a hostel, and was now stood in front of me in the activity centre we ran in the East End of London where Alan was a keen member of the art studio. He painted, he acted, he was a bit of a star around the place. Except today he was screaming, red faced and about to throw a table at my staff.

He had just done a bit of voluntary work for us and our member of staff wouldn't give him his lunch money because the receipt he brought back wasn't a receipt but instead a page ripped from a notebook with handwriting on it saying, "One Hamburger - 8 pounds". My staff member was a young lad in his twenties who hadn't long been out of college and he put his head on one side and in a very soft voice – so soft you could have put a flake in him and eaten him at the seaside – said, "Oh Alan, I know it's difficult to understand when you're homeless so I really do sympathise but you see a receipt from that café doesn't look like this, this looks like something you could have written – not that you would Alan I am sure because you're a good man – and also Alan I'm afraid a hamburger in that café doesn't cost £8". Alan got upset at this. So upset that he was making a lot of noise in the centre and everyone came out of all the different rooms to see what was going on. I was asked to come and talk to him. He was very pumped up and the veins in his neck were bulging. My staff were pretty shocked at what I said to him next and were very disappointed in me because Alan didn't calm down at all, in fact he stormed out of the centre into the night still angry. All I said was: "Alan you're a big man, I'm a big man and you and I know that you are taking the piss with this receipt. We'll pay your money when we get a real one, no problem. Now stop throwing chairs and piss off for tonight cos you're scaring everyone and you and me can have a good chat about it over a cuppa tomorrow morning alright?"

The thing is that Alan came back the next day and would only speak with me. When he found me he looked me in the eye, shook me by the hand and said, "Sorry man I was bang out of order yesterday." We had a cup of tea, sorted the receipt thing out and all was well.

I'm not advocating that we should all approach angry people and tell them to "piss off" but I knew Alan, I knew how we spoke to each other and that was me giving him respect, believe it or not. I was speaking to him exactly like I'd speak to any other grown up who was behaving like he was. I didn't put on my "voice for when speaking to a homeless person" whilst having my head on one side and basically treating him like a child. Alan could not have got through 20 years in the army and the same again on the factory floor without knowing what a receipt was. The problem wasn't the money; the problem was being patronised by a young kid who talked down to him. That tone ... that tilt of the head on one side "oh poor Alan, it's hard being homeless". That tone comes out naturally when people don't even realise it. It is the sound that betrays what they think of people.

So even if you're not saying what people want to hear, they will always appreciate the respect you gave them by the way you said it. You have to trust that, though they might storm off in the moment, they will turn up the next day having had time to reflect on who, that day, had actually shown them respect by speaking to them on the level. See earlier chapter "The 3rd Way to Deal With Difficult Behaviour."

So here is another small radical act you can all do to help the world. Sadly there is so much patronising talk directed at people in times of crisis that I have known many people over the years who've either given up on services altogether or just have a face that they wear when tolerating staff. They show them the face they need to in order to get what they want. So let's all think about the tone and the language we're using because the jargon and the slightly patronising tone are like harsh swearing in terms of the reaction they will get – they harm and hurt and repel people.

If you'll indulge me with one final tiny story to close this chapter. Yesterday I attended a celebration event at a funder's head office with lots of recipients of their grants. The day started with one of the grantee organisations being asked to stand up and give us all some guidance – with the aid of a Powerpoint slide – on how we should talk to one another during the day's event without causing "trauma". Odd way to start a celebration event I thought. They continued to tell us that we should not use language that excludes anybody in the room. That's good, I thought. Then half an hour later, the same people presented to the group the results of their funded programme and consistently used language like "Person-centred", "trauma-informed", "system change" and so on. A hand went up. A young man, one of the neurodivergent members of another grantee group, said "I thought you told us at the start of the day not to use language that excludes." I could've kissed him.

THIS IS A PUBLIC L...
ALL WELCOME C...

Public living rooms
from around the world
Virginia
U.S.A.

BLACKBURN

How is it that Blackburn is only 20 minutes from Burnley and yet the response to us couldn't have been more different! The crowd that poured onto our furniture in Burnley the instant we arrived was not present here. In Blackburn they spent most of the day sitting on the council's own bolted down benches, which lined the outsides of the little square where we were basing ourselves, watching, observing us warily, suspiciously.

Eventually some people wandered over and tried out the sofas. Some of my favourite moments on the streets are incredibly fleeting and light. In Blackburn a street cleaner challenged a police officer to a quick game of Connect Four. (I'm starting to think we should get commission for mentioning Connect Four so much.) They were only there for about ten minutes before they went back to work but I could just tell it had made their day.

One young woman in big pink sunglasses sat on our sofa and stared at something behind us. After a while a few of us became distracted by her fixed gaze and followed it to see what was so important. She was examining the cylindrical staircase that took people from the street to the multi-storey car park. Why was this so fascinating to her? Noticing our quizzical faces she explained: "My partner just painted that car park staircase." It was not a small staircase, to be fair. Silently, the fella from the mobile phone shop, an elderly shopper and I all nodded with expressions that said "impressive". She smiled proudly. She was wearing shorts so went on to tell us that the tag on her leg was to monitor drug and alcohol use. Apparently it can monitor her sweat. She's been sober three months and just got her three kids back. A fact delivered with a voice of sincere pride. The elderly lady gave her knee a pat and said, "well done mum." The mobile phone guy smiled at her too, gave a thumbs up then told us his break was over. Pink sunglasses told us she was feeling hopeful about the future.

Three burka-wearing Muslim young girls were standing about ten feet away but decidedly not joining us. However, they were giggling and smiling at us. When I smiled back and raised my eyebrows questioningly one of them excitedly pointed at our public living room and said: "It's like *Friends.*" With this they laughed out loud and ran off. That's nice, I said out loud. "No they mean *Friends* the TV programme," said Cath who was slurping on an iced coffee and had spent most of the day on the sofa with us. "They think the sofa set up is like 'Central Perk', the coffee shop where the friends all met up." "Oh," I said. "But we can still be friends," said Cath. "Thanks," I replied.

Alan in a cowboy hat riding a mobility scooter said he thought Camerados was a good idea and he'd wear our badge down the social club on Saturday. This was in fact all Alan said in the hour or so he sat with us. He was just "being" and doing it in the company of others. His scooter and his cowboy hat trundled down the street, past M&S and turned the corner and I quietly hummed the theme to *The Magnificent Seven* under my breath. "Take 'em to Missouri Matt," to quote another film entirely.

Some Camerados from the regular public living room in Blackburn popped down to say hello. They meet in a former pub (most have closed in the town now) and it is incredibly cosy and welcoming with people playing board games, picking out a tune on a battered old upright piano, making each other mugs of tea on what used to be the bar in the pub. The mix of people is great, all cultures and ages. People just chatting or sitting silently observing the room in contentment.

Public living rooms
from around the world

Blackburn

WE'RE ALL A BIT SHIT SOMETIMES

The idea that success is overrated and failure needs to be normalised.

You'd think with all the serial killer shows on Netflix the word we all fear the most is "death". I'd say it doesn't carry anywhere near the taboo of another word though, and that word is "failure".

It's a properly weird thing, but when you're talking to anyone and you mention failure they wince, squirm and seek to correct you in favour of the phrase "a learning experience". That seems to be a cop out to me. Sweep it under the carpet and call it "learning".

Of course it's learning, everything is learning, but if we dilute matters and rob failure of its power we don't fully learn. We badly *need* those hot under the collar, uncomfortable moments where we have totally cocked it up in order to never do it again. Except of course we will. Yet we won't have failed in the same way because our memory of that awful disaster means we will probably have tweaked something, which in my opinion is the essential and constant iteration we all need on the road to a big success.

At first I thought this was just an English phenomenon. As John Cleese's character Archie Leach says in *A Fish called Wanda* the worst thing to happen to an Englishman isn't death, it's embarrassment. However it turns out it is not just the English. The people in Sierra Leone who started a

Camerados public living room in Freetown did so because they were trying to counter the strong characteristic in Sierra Leonean men to never
admit failure. They wanted a specific place where it was ok to fail and
state it clearly.

It's surely an unhealthy approach, if you consider just how much perceived "failure" there is around the place. There are lots of things that just
don't work out.

The American Psychological Association (APA) estimates that 41% of first
marriages will end in divorce in the USA in 2024. And 60% of second marriages.[6]

In the UK around 4% of new businesses fail in their first year, 34% fail by
the end of their second year, and 50% fail within three years.[7]

The percentage of 17 year olds in the UK who fail their driving test is 44.2%.
Not far off half of them.[8]

So you'd think if we're so used to failure we might want to get better at
dealing with it and talking about it? I always ask audiences I'm speaking to
if they would put their hands up if they've ever been through tough times.
It won't surprise you to know all the hands go up. We all have bumps in
the road yet we determinedly talk like we're just gonna keep driving the
same speed and not think about how to brake, swerve and deal with them
when they happen.

You'll remember in the chapter about trust I told you about the crack addicts dressed as elves wrapping Christmas presents. I remember a drugs
worker taking me to one side before we began the business and pinning
me to a wall with the words: "I think this is grossly irresponsible. If his
business fails then these people could go and have a blowout and that
could cost them their life. You will have blood on your hands." He wasn't

6   Anna Miller, *Can this marriage be saved?*, https://www.apa.org/monitor/2013/04/marriage

7   Experian, https://www.experianplc.com/newsroom/press-releases/2023/half-of-all-
new-businesses-fail-within-three-years-of-opening

8   Dept of transport, https://assets.publishingservice.gov.uk/media/5a7eff81ed915d74e33f-
3c0d/young-car-drivers-2012.pdf

holding back. I told him what we would do if the business didn't work out on that first day. We'd come back, put the kettle on and piss ourselves laughing about how bad it was. Then we'd think about how to make it better on Day Two. If it failed on Day Two as well, then we'd come back and this time we'd bust out the biscuits, make *two* cups of tea and laugh till we were hoarse. We'd shrug our shoulders, dust ourselves off and again we'd talk about peoples thoughts on how to make it better. If failure kept happening then we'd probably get together and decide together this wasn't gonna work and head out for a good meal.

We would *normalise* failure. We wouldn't catastrophise it, which is what this drugs worker was doing. Instead of making every enterprise a potential life ending one, how about just having a go at something and if it doesn't work out well, never mind. It's not the end of the world.

In Camerados we have a badge that people love. There's a picture of it at the end of this chapter. It's our most popular bit of merchandise. It says:

"I'm a bit shit sometimes"

If people stand next to you on a bus or train and read it you can see their face change. They smile. Often they lean in and say to you, "Me too pal!". There's an instant connection, We're all a bit shit sometimes. That little bit of vulnerability brings the barrier down. We all relax. We also connect.

Imagine for a second if you wore a badge that said "I'm an outstanding success all of the time". How do you think people would receive you? You may have your own thing going and feel good about it all, but my gut is that most people wouldn't warm to you.

Yet on social media I feel like we're doing that all the time. We pout, look stunning, post endless pictures of ourselves and invite the world to comment on our outstandingness. Our amazing holiday, our children's sports' medals, our successful marriage. I've nothing against celebrating success – of course not – but is that the ONLY thing we can do? We wonder why our kids have breakdowns because what if they don't measure up next time – all those people saw my last success on Facebook, what will they think of me now? The overwhelming cumulative effect is one that makes those who aren't doing well feel pretty rotten. It sort of says "There's no room for you here". If there was a balance it would be fine but there isn't. That's the problem. Good news is great, we need more of it for sure; however, if that's all there is, then it's rough.

Of course there is negative stuff on social media but that tends to be kind of harsh criticism. None of us would speak to anyone like this. The normal discourse on social media is like speaking the way we do when somebody cuts us up in traffic. We yell through the windscreen at them. We fire off a comment because the person is not stood next to us. And this contributes to our massive problem with failure too. If you're going to get crucified on social media for making a mistake, then the fear of failure is paralysing. This is why politicians don't speak normally, they are always thinking about whether their words will be clipped and used out of context to bring them down in a torrid bunfight on social media literally in the next hour.

If people are allowed to fail they get better at stuff – simple. So what happens when the human race seems to have a pathological fear of it. The places I used to run for people struggling with life were like little microcosms of society and the world – people just trying to get good at life – and yet our main interactions with them always made the context clear that there was the presence of constant sanctions and penalties. If you were behind with your service charge payments or committed various misdemeanours on the premises we could, and often would, evict you. We would make you leave the homeless hostel to go on the streets. How many of you have some kind of performance review at work where someone says "Well you've not done well this month so we're gonna take your house!"? Yet taking away someone's housing is a standard penalty in the homeless sector. I've known drug and alcohol recovery projects too that have a "zero tolerance" policy to anyone found to be relapsing; it would result in immediate eviction. Have they met an addict? Relapsing is going to happen, and taking away their roof isn't going to get them back on the programme. So odd.

So therefore we create a society built on terror of failure and falling. The fines for any kind of infraction are heavy and of course heaviest on those who live on very tight margins where one penalty notice can sink you. However, there is very little wriggle room for understanding that in our system.

Maybe I'm being Scrooge-like about all this. Write to me and tell me: maff@Camerados.org.

HULL

Foxy sat down and didn't say much for a while. He had a thick, white mane of hair tied into a ponytail and his features were sharp, defined and would have made a great granite statue in a town square somewhere. He had a big presence, he carried himself in a way that said "here was a very capable man". He had a big blue hoodie on which said just one word "PEACE". I told him I was a life-long admirer of the Quakers but didn't have the courage to be one. The uncompromising pursuit of peace was daunting. He told me he knew what I meant. "I was blown up in Yemen and had my kneecaps smashed in Northern Ireland. I can't be doing with the blue blazer brigade on Remembrance Day. I'm not one of them."

He is a carer for his wife who has Huntington's disease and watches the same episode of *Casualty* again and again every night because she now has dementia as well and can't remember she's already watched it. He doesn't mind, it seems to make her happy. I asked him what he was doing at the weekend and he said he was coming into town cos there was a march by Patriotic Alternative (a group who follow far-right views on things like nationalism) and it's always good to engage in conversation with a fascist. I couldn't tell if it was a euphemism for "beat up a fascist" but I didn't think so; I believed he was all about peace.

We talked a lot about engaging with extreme views in order to see the human and give them a chance to change, a chance for progress. It has always troubled me that by saying public living rooms are for anyone people might read this as somehow condoning the racist who is allowed to come in. Yet If we "cancelled" them or expelled them we have just succeeded in getting them conveniently out of our sight to make us feel better, whilst at the same time creating an enemy with a legitimate grievance about exclusion and censorship. And yet expressing their views in a public space can cause harm in someone who is triggered or traumatised by them. But can words cause harm, is it not our responsibility to hear things and not be harmed? It's not easy.

"I'm going on the weekend cos they should see that people disagree and they should at least consider that, listen to others, not be in their own bubble of fascism, unchecked, unchallenged. If I ignore them or exclude them then they never get to hear my side of the story," said Foxy. "It's my town too. This is a mutual thing. I let you march, you let me disagree."

The mood lightened immediately as we were hit by a sudden invasion of kids on their way home from school who swept into the public living room on their bikes and leapt on the chairs and bean bags, filled our ears with loud banter and hit me with question after question about what we were doing. Foxy and I traded some old Tommy Cooper one liners and a few more modern Tim Vine classics thinking this would entertain them but the kids just stared back at us. "The advantages of simple origami are two-fold," I offered. "Went to the corner shop," said Foxy, "bought four corners." SIlence. One kid, freckled, filthy from break-time footie, looked at us with disdain. "Are you guys on acid or something?"

It was getting dark, Foxy had gone home to watch *Casualty*, again, so I started to pack up. I brought the van round and as I got out it started to rain. "Bugger," I thought, I was a bit tired and my back was hurting just looking at the sofas. Suddenly from the distance I saw a man leaping across the square towards me. Raphael was tall, handsome with a goatee beard, a beanie hat and an infectious smile and spirit. He spontaneously offered to help me carry the sofa back into the van before they all got wet. "Blimey, where did you come from! You're a lifesaver," I said. "You English," he laughed, "always so dramatic, it's a bit of rain and I'm a bit of help, no big deal come on let's go!"

Half-Polish, half-Greek, Raphael had fallen out badly with his parents and is now sleeping rough. He is very philosophical about it. "When we cannot avoid things we need to find joy somehow in the change and embrace it." We worked alongside each other, silently loading chairs, rugs, tables into the van, then carried either end of the sofas. The rain was coming down heavily now. Raphael didn't waver, he kept going. We chatted a little under the shelter of a bus stop when we'd finished. I offered him a coffee but he wouldn't accept. I pushed some money into his hand and told him it would be something that made me happy if I could thank him with something as small as a meal and a beer. He finally accepted graciously, we hugged and I drove off.

"When we cannot avoid things we need to find joy somehow in the change and embrace it." This was tumbling around my brain as the windscreen wipers pushed the swimming pool of water from my eyes on the M62 away from Hull. I didn't put the radio on, just listened to the rain and thought about Foxy, Foxy's wife and Raphael's damn phrase. The warmth and romance of his advice dissipated when I drove away and wondered which doorway he was currently residing in, wet and still homeless. Then when I pulled over for petrol I saw a message on my phone. Raphael was in a pub enjoying a meal and a nice beer and had enjoyed our meeting.

FAIRY LIGHTS MELT YOUR BRAIN

The idea that decor speaks

People have sneered sometimes at Camerados because of our love of fairy lights, comfy sofas and relaxed environments. I get quizzical looks when I suggest that fairy lights do something to the human brain (some of you may know these as "Christmas Lights"). However the neurological impact of staring at twinkling strings of lights is something I've witnessed time and again. When people see fairy lights, they do not expect to see a "Needs and Risk Assessment Form" popping in front of them anytime soon. You don't see fairy lights in a police station or a hospital. It sort of signals to you that you're in a different kind of place with a different vibe. People's brains tell them to kick off their shoes and relax, and that is what we've seen them do.

I saw the power of environments as I bumbled my way through my career in the social justice world. The first was a fairly extreme example. I managed to sweet-talk the government into giving me the biggest single-span building in the world – the Millennium Dome – and turn it into a homeless shelter for Christmas.

The Dome holds three billion cubic litres of air, cost £789 million to build and is now called the O2 arena where you and 20,000 other people can go see Justin Bieber perform while eating a Nando's as you play 10-pin bowling in front of a multiplex movie and buy a new iPhone. The place is huge.

We had 12 articulated lorries in the space taking away all our stuff and they looked like Tonka toys against the vast backdrop. I remember we would be fined £1,000 for every minute we stayed beyond our allotted time after the event, and just after the photo at the end of this chapter was taken I was pushing our last item out the door, which was a beautiful black grand piano on castors that weighed a ton (I'd been offered it so thought why not); I was being followed by a man with a clipboard counting down the seconds, shaking his head at me and wondering what the hell I'd been doing with a Steinway in a homeless shelter.

The Steinway and the Dome were all part of a feeling we had which was that we're going to confound homeless people's expectations and give them something fantastic that convinces them that they are worth it. Often you're sat opposite someone who has been let down by the system time and again, or has let everyone down themselves, and you're selling them an opportunity, a new hostel place, a flat, a college course, some kind of hopeful future and you're doing it whilst sat inside a total shit hole of a homeless project. Not surprisingly they think, "Why the hell should I trust you? Look where we are, all I deserve is this kind of crappy life in this kind of crappy place." So we wanted to deliver a major bit of "wow" and confound their expectations, make them think maybe seemingly impossible things could happen to me. Does that sound corny? I don't massively care cos it sounded utterly ridiculous when I told colleagues I was going to blag the Dome. And also I have a corny true story to prove it ... the first person through the doors of the Dome that year was an old homeless fella in a long brown coat and a flat cap and a very worried expression on his face. He looked around and broke into a smile and said, "Is this place really for me?" True story.

(As a little side story which is not relevant to anything but a good story, I had convinced the Coldstream Guards to come down after they'd finished changing the guard at Buckingham Palace and play all our homeless guests through the door of the Dome. The Metropolitan Police got wind of this and decided they would send 50 uniformed police officers down to supervise because apparently the world's biggest building, the world's press (who always cover our shelters opening) and the Coldstream Guards created a potent terrorist threat. There was no way I was going to let the first thing our guests saw when they arrived be a phalanx of coppers in Hi-Viz jackets standing round the door, so with great sadness I had to cancel the band from the guards. Shame, it would have been a helluva treat.)

Confounding environments became a bit of a thing for me for the next few years. After the Dome experience, I was headhunted by the Government and asked to run their England-wide capital programme for rebuilding homeless centres, day centres and hostels across England. There are too many stories to tell here; but let's just say it was like a lifetime's education in four very full-on years. It afforded me the huge privilege of travelling the length and breadth of the country and seeing almost every kind of centre and service that exists to help people at the sharp end. I got to see groundbreaking social enterprises as well as shockingly archaic night shelters. I saw homeless men and women designing their own gardens and building their own hostel and I saw desperate basement crypts with twenty people to a room and precious little light or ventilation.

I'll tell just one story. I'm in one of those basement crypts and talking to the manager. I said to him that maybe it would be good if we made the place a little nicer, separate rooms not dormitories, ensuite bathrooms, some dignity. The manager, a tall, clean-shaven suited man leant towards me and said, "You can't make the place too nice for them, they'll take advantage and they'll never leave." I didn't know what to say. I told myself that this fella comes to work every day to help homeless people, his heart must be in the right place, and so punching him in the face probably wasn't the right course of action, so I wandered off to talk to some folk in the shelter. I found a guy sitting in the shadows of one of the dark, dank underground rooms of bunks. He had a mass of hair and his face was filthy. I put the same proposition to him: wouldn't it be nice to have a place with separate rooms, more facilities etc. "No," he said, "this place is just fine for the likes of me, it's all we deserve buddy, these people are very good to me, it'll do just fine." And there you have it. If we lower people's expectations of what they deserve then they become complicit in the whole deal. They start to think of themselves as being worth less too.

The environment sends so many signals to people before anyone has opened their mouth to greet them. One of my biggest battles was with charities and councils who wanted to keep aggressive, glass-screen secure reception areas. It was the first thing people see when they arrive.

A glass screen instantly does two things: it makes the staff behind them feel they don't have to make much effort as nobody can get to them anyway; secondly, the person on the other side of the screen has to shout. So let's think one thing we might not want to encourage people to do when they arrive, homeless, in crisis, desperate through the doors of your hostel ... shout? And we wonder why reception areas are such a flash point. I would convince agencies to take the glass screens down and replace it with open hotel style reception areas. In one large day centre and hostel in the midlands, the staff walked out in protest because of the changes. I met with angry union officials and tearful staff apparently fearful for their lives now the screens were down. I made them an offer. I'd buy them a day out in London, I'd like to show them two projects there and then they could make up their own mind. One was a crazy busy day centre in the heart of the East End and one was a 190-bed hostel in Westminster. Both now had open reception areas. They spoke to staff there and discovered that violent incidents hadn't just reduced, they'd disappeared altogether. Why? Because human interactions happened in the reception, there was no glass to fight against, throw things at, shout through. The staff had to raise their game in diffusing tensions with people skills. Of course there are canny design features you can put into your open receptions to give you peace of mind if you need it. Have a long, wide, desk so by the time someone has clambered over it you are out the door. However, that didn't seem to be needed either.

Have you noticed there's lots of design in environments that is built on distrust? Like those shelves they put in train buffet cars, the ones that are sloped downwards, because they don't trust you to put away your cups in the bin so they design the whole environment to stop you putting it on a shelf. They'd rather you were uncomfortable than they had work to do. The plastic chairs in public buildings because why use fabric as you'll only tear it or spill something on it or piss yourself. The strip lighting so we can see what you are up to. I'm sure there is someone with a degree in facility management reading this and thinking of all the safety reasons for these. I would just ask them to consider the safety of creating hostile environments. If our environment can stir in us behaviours, then surely we want to decrease fear and anxiety in people? Wouldn't that be safer?

I would credit the environment of the Camerados public living rooms principally to the creativity of my colleague and lifelong friend, Jenny Fox. After six months of getting nowhere I realised that I am the only idiot who tries to start a movement about human connection on his own in his bedroom. I'd put some of my ideas out into the world, I'd met some brilliant designers who'd created a website and a cool brand but I wasn't getting anywhere. Then I landed a gig to work with some crack addicts in Blackpool so I went round for tea at my mate Jenny's house. She is the sunniest person I've ever known, amazing with people, a head for business (unlike me) and had run an award-winning social enterprise for homeless people, taking it from a tinpot operation to holding down major gardening and maintenance contracts. I knew she was on a career break. I knew that if we worked together her entrepreneurial gifts would make stuff happen. I also knew that people would be happier. Back then I tended to want everyone around me to be in a permanent state of outrage about the state of the world, whereas Jenny preferred dancing and cake. People were happier with the second option so I knew for Camerados we needed that in the recipe. It was Jenny who sat me down two years into Camerados and said, "Darling, everyone is pissed off at you" and called me out for developing classic "founders' syndrome" (it was my baby so I had an opinion on everything 24/7). You always need a brave friend around to call you out! After that, Jenny became the boss and ran the show much more effectively than I could and I did other stuff that played to my strengths. And I didn't piss everyone off so much! Anyway I digress horribly ... and so it was that Jenny's face fell when I showed her the first ever space for the first ever public living room. It was a mortuary.

Well, a former funeral parlour garage, to be precise. Where they parked the hearses. Our kitchen would be in the morgue where they put the bodies. It was a kind of squat come long loan to students who wanted to combat food poverty and create a food hall. They were inspiring young folk and felt that by partnering with us they might get it off the ground. They let us use their space and we bought them a boiler. They cooked pay-as-you-feel meals from surplus food provided by shops and we created a public living room – whatever the hell that was, we still didn't know.

The location was great, it was right in the centre of the city, and it helped that we were completely naive. For a start, we wanted to open it in January, when the temperature was below freezing. This was particularly a problem because the entrance had to be through an open garage door meaning that a whole side of the public living room would be open to the icy elements. And there was no heating. Oh and the only potential volunteers that we knew in the city were recovering alcoholics and students, not necessarily prized for their reliability, if you're feeling prejudiced. So all in all it didn't have raging success written all over it.

Despite all these challenges it was not a disaster, it was a bloomin' miracle. I really think a lot of the heavy lifting was the environment we created. I often bullshit people in important meetings by talking up our environments as if they were designed meticulously over years, perhaps by expert architects and anthropologists, in white offices with CAD drawings and multiple focus groups and intense studies. In fact Jenny pretty much invented the whole thing by going to Wilko's.[9]

Back then we didn't even have money for Wilko's, so Jenny said we should all have a look in our attics. Naturally this led to everyone getting down their Christmas decorations and Boom!, the fairy lights revolution was born. We put them everywhere and instantly the garage felt a lot cheerier. Then we went on Freecycle. If you can get your hands on a van, you can get furniture for free every day of the week. People don't want the hassle of getting sofas out of the house so if you'll pick them up you can have them. Pianos are the same. A student volunteer who dressed like every member of Earth, Wind & Fire offered to be our Freecycle scrounger and collector but he got a little carried away. We ended up with 14 sofas and pianos. We put one of the upright pianos on the pavement and I started playing it. We put the coffee on and Jenny sweet-talked people into lending blankets and hot water bottles – anyone walking in would be offered one.

The decor ultimately reflected Jenny's personality. It was warm, unpretentious, disarming and put everyone at their ease. She used linen tablecloths, NOT paper or gingham ones, and put real flowers in glasses on the tables sourced from florists who were throwing them out. She bought paper lanterns and hung them off string which lowered the ceiling height, then she filled the lanterns with battery-operated fairy lights. Throws and

9   Sadly no longer with us. Wilko's was a much loved cut-price homeware store.

cushions were draped on crappy mismatching sofas and rugs covered the concrete floor. She got a mate of ours to paint a brilliant mural on the wall that spoke to our mission and we had chalk boards outside – more on them in another chapter, but needless to say they got people to come in.

We couldn't believe how well it worked. Fiona, who kipped in the doorway opposite, used it because she was too afraid to use homeless services. I remember seeing her one day happily chatting away to two young yuppies who carried Louis Vuitton luggage and a large Nikon camera. They were passing through and thought our place was "cool and boho". There were builders in Hi-Viz jackets having a cuppa laughing with shoppers laden down with bags from the city centre. A few doors down from our entrance there was both a mental health drop-in centre and a drugs advice centre. Both of them started bringing their clients up to our public living room for their key-worker meetings because they preferred our crap old sofas and armchairs to their expensively kitted out professional office and interview rooms.

The system seems surprised that a nice place matters. Everybody seems perfectly content for schemes to be horrible, institutional places. Perhaps they think it is a budgetary thing, but that doesn't stack up. I remember a manager of a women's hostel in Liverpool who took tiny amounts of money out of petty cash and bought a few plants and vases and some cheap paintings in frames from charity shops. He dotted them along the corridors and hey presto it felt more homely like someone gave a damn and wanted you to relax.

Here's another weird thing. Think about all the places we might go in times of personal crisis – the police station, the hospital, the council offices. Do the names of these places conjure up images of warm comforting environments? Do you think of them and instantly imagine being put at ease? Don't you think that when you're at your most anxious it might be a good idea not to create places that just amplify the fear?

We all think about what kind of environment we're creating in other spheres, both personal and professional, but for reasons I've never wholly understood, we don't think about it for people going through hell.

The first public living room in Sheffield. Before then after ...

191

First Ever
Public Living Room
Before and after

192

LIKE NO PLACE ON EARTH

The idea that mixing with people who are not like you makes everything better.

There were many things we learnt from turning that funeral parlour into a public living room in that cold month of January but unquestionably the discovery that convinced us this idea had legs was that we had never seen such a mix of people in the same space before.

I had all sorts of theories at the time about why there was this crazy mix of people in that very first public living room.

One involved representation. In the early days, when we felt public living rooms had to be manned, we recruited volunteers and, as I said above, they were principally from two places: the University of Sheffield student body and an organisation that worked with people who had alcohol problems, who ran a rehab and programmes around addiction. I walked in one day and behind the counter serving coffee was Alexandria, a student of Italian and Spanish literature who looked like the Lady of Shallott, and Paul, an alcoholic ex-plumber whose face looked like the proverbial bag of spanners. The pair giggled together as they served up coffee and biscuits and to me this gave one clear message to anyone passing by: "Come in, everyone is welcome here."

Another was the signage. We didn't hang a sign on the door saying "Lone-liness and isolation café". We knew enough to know that would be a turn off. So instead we put a black board up and wrote in chalk:

"TOP FIVE DAVID BOWIE SONGS

1. Heroes

2. Life on Mars

3. Gene Genie

4. Starman

5. Let's Dance

COME IN AND ARGUE!"

As a result we had all sorts coming over and commenting. A builder in Hi-Viz getting tearful about having "Heroes" played at his dad's funeral; a very animated old rocker saying "'Let's Dance' was too poppy for Bow-ie"; people picking up the chalk and wiping off titles and putting down "Young Americans" or whichever song they felt was sorely missing from the list. These people drifted in on the basis of conversation, not cos they felt the place was their client group or brand or whatever. They came in as humans, otherwise known as Bowie fans. Other days we put different bands up or movies or even some more contentious stuff. "Favourite Tory Politicians" was a memorable one, certainly for Sheffield.

Maybe it was the signs, maybe the fairy lights and decor, maybe the piano, maybe it was Paul and Alexandria, who knows, but whatever it was this wasn't a place that required a social passport depending on what you earn and what you look like. The effect was an atmosphere that is really hard to put down on the page. I've felt it sometimes in a football stand on match day or maybe in a train carriage when the train guard is feeling jovial and joking with everyone, that sense of collective experience. It's something in the air, a feeling of common humanity. Nobody says it out loud, they just sense it and they join in. That last bit is crucial, people sense the com-mon humanity and step up to meet the challenge: they chat to strangers.

In that funeral parlour that became the world's first public living room, we naturally didn't have a clue what we were doing, so we asked people to leave post-it notes and postcards to tell us what they thought of the place, give us ideas and inspire others. I remember one that said:

"I had a miscarriage last week. I haven't told anybody about it. I feel very sad. I keep setting off to work but turning back. I chatted to some strangers here and it just gave me a bit of confidence. I'm off to work now. Thanks very much for this place."

One man left us a note. It said:

"This is better than my living room, in fact it's more functional."

... and so this thing we created had a name: Living Room. We added the 'Public' later. As with many things we do, we shoved something out there and people told us what it was, helped us understand it and then told us what it was called. Crazy to think that from that garage in Sheffield there are now public living rooms all over the country and now dotted around the world.

Our next public living room was in a library in Blackpool. In that way we had a head start because a library is that special in-between kind of public space. The public realm tends to be divided into places that sell you stuff and places that fix you. A public living room aims to be neither and a library is the closest thing to it already out there. People can just go to a library and "be". It's also not particularly identifiable with any particular group or demographic so anybody and everybody goes there. We used the same philosophy as in Sheffield and the mix just got even greater with more and more people coming into the library to go to the public living room and spend their day there.

People seemed to notice the mix of people and began to protect everyone's right to use it. An extreme situation happened when an old man who was known locally to be a convicted sex offender came into the Blackpool public living room, which by then was also a café with staff who we employed. One of our employees was a passionate young man who lived in a homeless hostel and whose multiple piercings, tattoos and history of violence belied his love of baking bread. As a father who was only allowed to see his beloved son once a week with supervision, he had sworn that if he ever saw the sex offender again he'd "cut him and kill him". However, after months of helping us run the public living room something must have changed in him because when the old man reappeared one day something remarkable happened. Noticing the anxiety the old man's presence was causing some customers with children, the young man bent down and whispered in the man's ear asking him if he wouldn't mind coming back a few hours later, whereupon they could have a coffee together. The old man smiled and said that was no problem and duly wandered off. We asked the young man why the change and he said, "Well in here we mix with people who aren't like us don't we?"

We had another extraordinary example of this strange atmosphere in the pop-up we did inside a gallery space in Rotherham. It was popular among some lads from the local homeless hostel and also some asylum seekers supported locally by the British Red Cross. After a while we discovered that one of the homeless lads was an active member of the English Defence League, a far-right group that regularly marched in the town. He was starting to open up the public living room in the mornings and tidy the place along with a young man called Yacoob who was black and from Sudan. As they set the tables out in the morning, fluffed the cushions, warmed up the urn and put some tunes on, the two became friends. During Black History Month we asked them to run a Camerados stall together, which they did.

I want to tell you about two examples of how this mix thing has worked elsewhere in the world.

In the east side of Tokyo, it's Monday morning and children are arriving a little cranky after the weekend, not really in the mood to attend their nursery and say goodbye to their parents. Then suddenly their faces light up and they skip through the gates. Waiting for them are groups of elderly people, some of them six decades older and some in wheelchairs. The elderly people's faces light up too. Little hands are placed inside wrinkly ones and they go inside together. This is Kotoen[10], a community-based integrated care centre for children and the elderly.

10   Azreen Hani, *Kotoen: Intergenerational living at its best*, *The Malaysian Reserve*, https://themalaysianreserve.com/2019/12/23/kotoen-intergenerational-living-at-its-best/

It was sort of created by accident by its founder Shimada Masaharu when renovations were needed and the nursery and old people's home had to share facilities. It took an open mind and an observant one to notice that mixing these two groups actually made something magical happen. The *Japan Times* wrote: "The benefits soon became apparent. Seniors found a solution to the loneliness and boredom that characterised so many nursing centers. According to a study in 2013, seniors began smiling and conversing more among themselves. Moreover, they exhibited delayed mental decline, lower blood pressure and reduced risk of disease and death compared with seniors in non-participating facilities. But the program is not a one-way street by any means. Toddlers developed respect and empathy for the elderly, which enhanced their social and personal skills."[11]

In 1999 the legendary conductor, musician and music icon Daniel Barenboim brought to life an idea he had with his friend the Palestinian writer and teacher Edward Said. They felt music could play a role in healing perhaps the most intractable divide on our planet, that between Israelis and Palestinians, the Arab and Jewish peoples.

They held a small music workshop that grew into an orchestra consisting of equal numbers of Arab and Israeli musicians. Others from Spain, Iran and Turkey joined the ensemble too. Every summer they meet for rehearsals and then go on an international tour playing the greatest concert halls of the world. The idea is to promote "coexistence and intercultural dialogue".[12]

The orchestra was named after Goethe's "West-Eastern Divan", an astonishingly prescient collection of poems written between 1814 and 1819, which represents something that still eludes us two centuries later — a real exchange of ideas between Christian and Muslim.

Edward Said died in 2003 but left us these words:

11   Walt Gardner, *Interaction benefits toddlers and elderly alike*, Japan Times, https://www.japantimes.co.jp/opinion/2016/03/13/commentary/japan-commentary/ interaction-benefits-toddlers-elderly-alike/

12   https://west-eastern-divan.org/divan-orchestra

"Separation between peoples is not a solution for any of the problems that divide peoples. And certainly ignorance of the other provides no help whatever."

Both these projects showed that mixing very different kinds of people created hugely positive experiences and a big impact on people's lives. However, somebody slammed these groups together in an "innovative" project. It didn't happen naturally. And that's because it doesn't. We all self-select where we drink, shop, eat and therefore who we mix with. Maybe in a train station you get a mix of everyone, but it's rare. I mentioned earlier that I am a lifelong devotee of particular places where I have always felt incredibly at home and it's probably because of the natural mixing that just happens there. I'm talking about the great American Diner and the great British caff. You can find anyone and everyone there, often at any hour of day or night, feasting on a ridiculous array of delights. They are havens for misfits and regular folks and there are no airs or graces. Maybe my personal obsession with these places fed subliminally into the creation of public living rooms.

This gets complicated when identities are important to people. It is hugely valuable to people to belong to a self-help group focused around their condition, for instance. You can talk openly about very personal issues knowing others will understand because they have been there too. This is hugely comforting, informative and valuable.

A major inspiration for Camerados was the global movement Alcoholics Anonymous. AA has been going since 1935 and there could be 10 meetings happening in your neighbourhood tonight without you knowing it. In each meeting, strangers will come together without judgement and share their most personal stories. They will support each other without being each other's friends. They will contribute to the hire of the room – those who can afford to – then go their separate ways. I know there are various aspects of AA that people don't like and I may agree, but purely in the way it functions, it's a beautiful model and there's nothing to stop it going for another 85 years.

But these people are brought together through a shared condition: alcoholism. The anonymity and trust comes from a strong bond of shared experience. There are similar groups with strong supportive bonds meeting in community venues every night across the globe based around shared medical conditions, shared trauma, shared family issues and the list goes on. Membership of a club gives a huge sense of belonging and purpose. There are tens of thousands of unconstituted groups in the UK alone, people in knitting clubs, book groups and the like, giving up hours to be with others in a collective pursuit. The person getting up at 6am to paint white lines on a football pitch where children play their weekend matches isn't getting paid, but it's their role at the club so they are happy to do it.

So please do not misunderstand me, there's strength in similarity. We just think there's space for another place too. A place that doesn't really exist.

A place where truly everyone can come in, because consider this: Do any of the following things unite all people of all persuasions? Religion. Politics. Sport. Music. Fashion. Health conditions. Drinking alcohol. Cooking. Knitting?

They do not. No judgement on all of them, we know these things can bond people very strongly and meaningfully together. The point is that they also have the power to divide, marginalise and exclude. Perhaps what we're trying to do with public living rooms and Camerados is create a place of shared experience where the shared experience is *life*. Humans coping with the ups and downs on planet earth. Camerado is a term that could just as easily be the word "human".

NOTTINGHAM

We start the day in an area called Hyson Green which shows up on every indicator as an area in Nottingham with "challenges" and I'm feeling challenged today too. Confidence is a fickle mistress and comes and goes for reasons I don't fully comprehend. This morning for some reason I don't quite have it and so can't bring myself to plant the furniture in front of the bed shop on the corner where I really want to go. So I go inside to buy blankets from them and hopefully win over the proprietor with my purchase and pop the question about blocking his shop windows. I bottle it again and come out with forty quids worth of garish, fairly awful blankets and no solution to my problem. So I notice there's an empty shop, with piles of litter on the ground outside it, further up the road and not in such a prominent spot, but I shake off my prevarication and unload the van. My brother and his daughters turn up, they live in the city, and give me a hand. Their company gives me a big boost.

We can't get the public living room banner to stay up so I go looking for some Gaffer tape (in life, after a cup of tea, there are few greater essentials than Gaffer tape. Never leave home without it. But don't ever say that to people because you sound like a serial killer). Right beside us in the opposite direction from the bed shop is a fruit and veg shop. It has a huge frontage with stunningly presented fresh produce on display. The owner stands outside and his sons cluck around the store busily. He is a handsome Pakistani gentleman and he says to me, "I like this thing you are doing. Very nice." I thank him and ask him if he knows where there is a shop I can buy Gaffer tape. He directs me inside and I say, "No, I need Gaffer tape" and he nods and again points inside. To humour him I wander into his grocery store in no hope of finding cloth tape with strong adhesive and tensile properties popular in the industrial staging world. And yet this shop has a choice of three colours. Yes, only in a Pakistani food market can you find absolutely everything you are looking for. The inside of the shop was huge with multiple aisles and proof that Tesco's were not the first to stock everything you need; Pakistani corner shops got there first.

"He can tell you if you've got a good soul," says the woman whose enormous brown bulldog – seriously the size of a lion – has taken up residency on one of our sofas, stretching out so there is no room for puny humans. "Also he'll eat you if you don't." We laugh nervously and lean back and away from the pooch.

The owner is a blonde middle-aged woman wearing mostly black and being very casual and confident and throwing her sentences at us while looking somewhere else. "I like company but when I swim in the River Trent I can't stand those wild swimming clubs." She pulls a face and slumps her body over. "Menopausal women bossing me around, telling me to wear a swimming cap in case my body drifts downstream. I mean for god's sake I'm a whale, they'll find me!"

A fella walks up to us and shyly asks if he can sit down. We wave him in and he joins our band of misfits that morning. "Is that you Paul?" says my brother and wanders over to him to give him a warm handshake. Turns out Paul used to beg outside my brother's local Sainsbury's and they'd chat from time to time. He has just kicked a 20-year crack habit and is now working in a care home. "That's great," says my brother, "I'm so chuffed to hear that." Paul lights up. He tells us he is the only white member of staff and it's run by a Muslim charitable organisation. He says they are very kind to him and it helped him get off the streets by being a job that comes with sleep-in accommodation. He enjoys the work, he has a real connection with a lot of the old folks and it makes him feel good to work so hard for them. He eats from the canteen and they serve amazing curry meals most of the time. As nice as the people are, he says he doesn't really fit in but he's grateful to them for the job.

"Would it surprise you to know that outside of work this is the first time I've chatted in a group of normal people?" We all smile and my brother says, "Sorry to disappoint you there Paul but we're not normal mate, we're all mad and weird."

Andy arrives and the moment he does Paul leaves with just a wave good-bye. It's only later that we realise it's because Paul probably knew Andy from the streets and there's some history there. Andy has something to say. He has just walked out of a homeless hostel to live on the streets again.

"They don't have to talk to me like that. And they don't have to tell every-one all my personal stuff." He had a good rant about how the hostel staff treated him like a child and he had his dignity. We chatted about this a bit and then we moved off his problems and debated movies and favourite actors. Andy seems to know a lot about topics for which people pick me for their pub quiz team, unless that is, my brother Si is available. So today he and Andy are out of my league.

Later on in the day we move location to the city centre and the big Plaza outside the town hall. Lots of people stop by, they play cards, drink tea, get out their guitar. It's like a party atmosphere and then suddenly we see Andy again. He sits down and says, "I've gotta thank you lot."

"I decided to challenge the hostel staff. They agreed with me and have got me a place somewhere else where I know I really like the staff. Honestly folks I don't think I'd have done that if I hadn't spent the day talking to nice people. It just put my confidence up a few notches so thanks for that." We told him it had been a mutual thing and his company had made our day. For me, that was certainly true. My day on Nottingham's street had sorted out the confidence wobbles I felt that morning and my own black dogs retreated thanks to wild swimming dog owners, Pakistani gaffer ta-ble purveyors, Andy "pub quiz brain" and everyone else who had my back that day.

CAN YOU DISAGREE WELL?

The idea that if I disagree with you I don't have to hate you

It's awkward as a Brit to hear from a friend that they voted differently from you on Brexit, it feels like a divide of values that can't be bridged. If you're American maybe that's how you feel as a Trump supporter watching cable shows lampooning you as an intellectually challenged hillbilly. Maybe you're a trans person being asked about JK Rowling. How do you feel about Just Stop Oil protesters believing nobody is facing the truth about our planet, versus the people in cars on the M25 below just wanting to get to work. Do you feel comfortable supporting Israel? I could go on and on obviously. It certainly feels there are more subjects likely to be social dynamite and divide people more than any other time I have lived through.

Occasionally in my team we run little campaigns to remind folk of some of our principles and both their essential yet confounding nature. The year I write this book is special in the entire history of humankind, in that never have so many people in the world gone to the polls. So, on top of all the little conversational minefields mentioned above, you now have a media chock full of everyone shouting and screaming to get your attention for their differing points of view. You could call this healthy and wonderful, the freedom to do so being obviously very precious. It is, yet it can also feel like a lot of stress both to figure out what you think and feel and also how to talk to each other about it without feeling uncomfortable being shouted at. So we held a campaign called "Dunk Off: Let's get ready to Crumble!".

We asked people to sit down with somebody they knew that they disagreed with. We asked them to talk about a different topic on which they might disagree a little less (preferably something silly) whilst dunking a biscuit of their choice into their brew ("brew" being an English term for a cup of tea, but of course any hot drink was allowed!). The person whose biscuit fell into their brew first lost the contest!

And so it was that in public living rooms and other places too people sat down awkwardly with people to discuss whether it is ever OK to have fish on pizza. Or worse, pineapple? Should you ever pee in the shower? Who is your favourite muppet? I can tell you that after hundreds of these contests there is a general consensus that digestives are pretty good dunkers, ginger nuts too. Hobnobs tend to disappoint, as do Jaffa Cakes. There was much laughter and though the big topics were never discussed they saw each other as human and the ice between them thawed a bit. In one famous instance, a local member of parliament walked into a public living room and sat down with one of his constituents who cannot stand him. The constituent had almost left the moment they saw them enter but instead was persuaded to take part in a "Dunk Off". They didn't resolve the "fish on pizza" debate but they did laugh and leave on good terms. That was all it took to thaw the constituent's enmity. He now saw his enemy as a human.

One thing we stipulated to everyone was that the point of "Dunk Off" was not to reach any agreement of any kind. Imagine that? You don't have to agree! Weird how so much of the pressure is released by that, as if society forces us to demand that in every social interaction. The point was to sit down with someone you disagreed with and just spend time in each other's company, and for it to be OK. Obviously there are big values-based issues that drive us apart, but very often it's just smaller things that make things very awkward suddenly for us to sit together and we tend to remove ourselves. It's a real shame, as one Camerado said to me very recently: "If people disagree with me I just think what's the point in me sitting here." It's as if being disagreed with is the same as "you have no worth".

I would say that this issue is the biggest thing people have struggled with in our movement after the "no fixing" principle. In an era where people are "cancelled" or "de-platformed" it is not always popular to encourage people to sit down with a racist or a sexist. Naturally it's a given that we shouldn't put ourselves in a position of harm but surely we have to model a world where exchanging views is positive not harmful?

I remember one woman taking me to task on a big Zoom call. We have these "Open House" video calls where anybody around the world can zoom in and give us their ideas and thoughts, support or challenge, on what we're doing. It's our attempt at being led by the movement itself and sometimes five people show up and sometimes 20, sometimes more. There seems to be no rhyme to it. Back in the pandemic days we got big numbers and, on one of these calls where there were about 50 present, a woman told us we were not meeting her needs. She said that we hadn't assessed what she needed and tailored the call accordingly and therefore this wasn't a "safe space" for her. I acknowledged what she said but answered that like our living rooms this is a "public" space and just a gathering of humans believing in an idea, we weren't a service, and as such don't profess to be meeting everyone's needs. She told me this was not good enough. At this point someone spoke and left a lasting impression on us all. A trans man called Alfie turned his mic on and said: "For God's sake please don't meet all my needs in Camerados." Everyone froze (not literally and not on Zoom either, we just were spellbound). Alfie continued to tell us about how his life has lots of groups based around different aspects of his life – his gender, his neurodivergence and so on – "but I come to Camerados to be accepted around all humans, where I can be different and nobody gives a toss."

Alfie put rocket fuel in us that day. We're still running on it. He made us want to work hard every day to make sure that the world wasn't just divided into safe spaces and unsafe spaces, but places where you could be together with everyone and rub along OK because we didn't give a toss if we disagreed with one another, we still had each other's back and would look out for one another. Thanks Alfie.

When I was reading Srdja Popovic's book (mentioned in an earlier chapter, *Blueprint for Revolution*) I turned over one of the last pages and read a sentence which stopped me in my tracks. It said: "Here is my personal email address, contact me if you want to change the world, I *will* get back to you." I couldn't believe it. I'd never read a book where the author said, "Do you want to meet?". Having had my mind totally rocked by the pages I had read up to that point, this was a punch in the stomach, I was also overwhelmed to be addressed by him directly. I confess I got a bit emotional and scared. I put off contacting him for a couple of years because I felt we hadn't done enough yet. Then one day, on a trip to New York to visit some Camerados out there I finally thought I'm gonna do it, and I wrote him an email.

Then nothing. It was just a stunt, I thought, how silly and naive I was to expect a reply. Then it came. His name was in my inbox. His email apologised for his tardy response, telling me that his team had to check me out first because Putin's thugs had been attacking his staff. The team had done a check on me and told him, "I have to meet this guy cos he's doing amazing stuff." I gulped. He was kind, wrote at length how much he admired our work and said he was in the UK the following week lecturing at the University of Essex, and that's how we came to meet in the back of a pub in Colchester.

He walked in, saw me at the bar and walked towards me with his arms open asking for a hug. After three hours of laughter and deep chats, I asked him to sign a copy of the book that had such a life-changing effect on me. Little did I know how prophetic and ominous his inscription would be. He used a phrase I'd never heard before, it felt a little clunky but then English is not this guy's first language so I didn't think about it. Remember this is in 2017. It read:

"Maff, the answer to everything is to reduce the social distance between people."

Social distance? Odd phrase. Never heard it before. Fast forward three years and it became law in almost every country on the planet – overnight – to increase social distance between people. We always had that problem. We have always increased the social distance between ourselves and people with whom we disagree. I think this is a problem we are still living with and our work is needed more than ever.

DUNK OFF
CAMPAIGN

209

BRIGHTON

Sofas and armchairs are hardly an aggressive act, but putting them on pavements without permission can still get me into trouble with some scary confrontations and awkward moments, so every time I climb in the van to head to a street I do get a little flurry of nerves in my stomach. I've also witnessed my brain start to send me the same thoughts: "It looks like it might rain, maybe today's not the day for it"; "You have done so many of these now maybe today is the day you just head home, you've done enough"; "Not sure if it'll work in this town." I think this is probably common to many activists. Your brain is trying to talk you out of it, to give you easy excuses. I enjoy noticing it when it happens and I know I just have to push through it, and it's always worth it. The nerves are useful, they keep you on your toes, and they make work a little bit more exhilarating. A bit of mischief has certainly kept the fire in my belly and made me feel like I'm achieving something, which we all need in our work.

However, there are times when pushing through the nerves can lead to a bit of cockiness. Like in Brighton for instance when I thought, "What the hell" and just drove the van directly onto the famous pier. I got as far as putting the big rug down and the sofa at the very entrance to the pier when I heard walkie talkies crackle all around me. "I've got eyes on him," I heard a voice say on a radio. "On my way," said another, which I presumed belonged to the enormous man who now stood over me, black uniform, stab vest, assorted security credentials. He just pointed at my public living room and said, "I don't think so". I beamed at him and said, "Ah come on it's a nice thing!" "I'm sure it is mate but this is private property and you can't do it. I gotta get you to move." "Ok no worries," I said and started folding up the rug. I think the security guard, who's name is Ebrima, was surprised at this, he expected more of a fight. "I tell you what," Ebrima offers, interrupting my packing up, "if you go just over there where the tarmac changes colour from red to black, that's not our land and I don't need to do anything with you then." I tell him that he didn't have to be that nice and I appreciate it and then he tells me to get the other end of the sofa and he helps me carry it to the black tarmac. At this point he sits down on the sofa and says, "I'm on a break now can I spend it with you?" At this point two women from a local community organisation stop by to say hello – they're fans of Camerados – and they sandwich Ebrima in the middle of them on the sofa. He is loving this and stays for quite a while just shooting the breeze.

One of the two women had been on the streets with me the day before when we popped-up the public living room outside a co-op in White-hawk, an area on the West side of Brighton and one famous for its deprivation and difficulties.

Local resident Janet stops to talk to us when she pops to the co-op for her morning newspaper and pint of milk. We end up in great discussion about the so-called "Cost of living crisis" and how it does feel very real for some folks. "I feel sorry for my sister-in-law and her big house with a swimming pool," Janet says, to the disbelief of the builders in hardhats who are eating their lunch with us. "She has to heat the bloody thing! I live in a pokey little spot up the road in Whitehawk but it's lovely and warm. Who's laughing now eh?!"

Shortly after this a woman called Pat zooms up at speed on her purple mobility scooter. In her early seventies with limbs that let her down she announces to me, "I get plenty of attention from young men." She also told me that she'd just got back from hospital. "They don't listen to me and I can't get a bloody appointment, never. But I control pain, it doesn't control me?" "How?" I asked. She pointed at her bobble hat, "My mind."

Back on the pier an American gentleman from Washington DC in his sixties stands and stares at us. "I think I have found my home," he says. Everyone smiles and offers him a seat. He tells us that he has planned his whole trip to Europe around a celebration he is attending that afternoon at a pub up the road. It is called "The Bevy" and it is owned and run by the community. Unlike most community owned pubs it is not in a wealthy area and it has lots of amazing activities for a community with challenges. There is a disability disco, breakfast club for families where food is scarce, job clubs and loads more. "Well I'll see you there" I say "because the celebration event is also the launch of their new public living room." The man laughs. "What a coincidence we should meet!"

We spent a wonderful afternoon with our friends at "The Bevy." After all, the pub is the original public living room.

CONCLUDING CHAPTER: SIT DOWN AND DON'T BE COUNTED

The idea that it's up to you!

The famous phrase "Stand up and Be Counted" is the evocation I want you to take away at the end of this book, the "call to arms" bit. I just really don't want you to take up "arms". And I'd really rather you didn't stand up. Or be counted.

Sit down with people, forge relationships, preferably with someone you disagree with. And don't worry too much about the data, the counting, the perceived success of what you're doing. Don't bother about giving "the man" any numbers, just do it because, well, you believe in it and it's the right thing to do.

A nurse said that to me once. She said, "This Camerados stuff reminds me of the 'sit on the end of the bed and chat to patients' thing we used to do. We shouldn't do it cos we're supposed to, we should do it cos it's just always been good to do it". It's so easy to get caught up in the cycle of doing something because our funder or our customer requires it, your boss says so, your performance review demands it, or your own measure of success needs it. Don't forget the stuff in the cracks. It's often the real stuff.

I'd love you to take away from this book that making a difference, making the world a better place, it doesn't have to be loud and shouted through a megaphone. Person to person, something tiny, day to day. Wouldn't you prefer a real little difference to your day than a cool slogan? Not filling the kettle quite so much saves the planet a little when multiplied by millions; well the same goes for looking out for someone and not being quite so much of a dick. Making a small change can make a big change.

I had better close this book before I choke on my own aphorisms or open a shop of inspirational posters.

So I guess I'm supposed to write a neat concluding chapter that ties everything together and gives you work to do. But this isn't school. I'd really much rather you figured out for yourself what this all means. Did the stories from the pavements connect with you at all? Did the things I've learnt over the years strike a chord?

Ok what have I been trying to say in all these pages?

Well I hope you've enjoyed meeting the wonderful people I met on the streets and that their stories have illuminated something about humanity for you. I hope it encourages you to pause your day occasionally for a chat with a stranger, it can be a deeply wonderful thing, for both of you.

And as for the "confounding ideas" that I put in the other chapters, I hope they are of some use to you in your daily life, your work, your community or even some big change you want to make in the world.

What connects all of the ideas is a drive to be more human and connect better with people, more mutually. I hope they help you navigate tricky situations and tricky days.

So to recap I guess I have to ask you some questions ...

Are you attending to the Meaning of Life in YOUR life?

It was in the title of the book, surely you didn't miss it?! I'm sure you could have got it from scholarly study but for me it was just being a witness to people on the precipice of life for thirty plus years. Friends and Purpose came out loud and clear, they were the pieces that were missing, and the pieces people cared most about. And the people who turned their life around made sure they had both. I hope that's handy to know. You're welcome! Please make your cheques payable to "MaffStartsNewReligionForTaxPurposes.com".

Are you persuaded that you need some human connection with your lasagne in times of crisis?

As if to demonstrate how blind we all are to the meaning of life we ignore it when we most need it. We push people away when we hit hard times – maybe out of anger, guilt or shame – but if your "duvet day" isolation becomes habitual, well then it's a problem. Maybe you'll think about that next time some crisis hits your neighbourhood or community and watch out for the people hiding away. Maybe accompany your lasagne with a personal visit and a chat? Food is easier, quicker and requires less investment of time. Connection can seem harder, conversations take longer. However, after the food, in a few hours, people are hungry again, whereas that conversation can keep them going for days. It can restore faith, lift confidence, alter someone's course and yes, even eventually change their life.

Will you think about the value of having more "weak-ties" – aka Camerados – in your day? And could you be one to other people?

None of the people that I met on the streets, that I wrote about in this book, were my "friends" as such. They were, as Wayne put it, "halfway between a stranger and a friend". These loose connections are missing for so many of us and yet they are so important in getting us through a tough day or a tough time. We've invented this term "Camerado" but call it whatever you like, there should just be more in the world.

Next time someone is upset, are you gonna join the No Solution Revolution?

Can you resist the urge to fix? Are you gonna notice when you next dive in with "What you wanna do is ..." when talking to someone? Can you find it within you to ask questions instead? That's all I've done in this paragraph so I'm gonna stop now before it gets annoying.

Will you recognise Bad Kindness next time you see it or next time you do it?!

No puppies were harmed in the writing of that chapter. I know it's not a popular argument but please consider how bad we make people feel with our acts of charity sometimes and take a second to think "Is this more about me than them?"

Can you remember the 6 most powerful words in the English language?

If all else fails, this rarely does. Ask someone struggling to do you a favour, it can be anything from advice to something mundane or whatever. It just rewires the situation, brings them out of the tunnel of their own problems a bit and gives them a jolt of purpose. Conveys trust, respect, value, belonging ... quite magic really.

Will you watch your language?

Words have power and not the ones we may think. Jargon words can be very useful in scholarly documents for encapsulating difficult concepts, but if we use them with humans, in the everyday, we have to accept that people – people you may really want to engage, to think, to change their behaviour – will switch off, feel excluded, judged even. It just won't achieve the impact you want. Maybe let's try to speak like a person, not a document.

Will you let yourself be a bit shit sometimes? And show others they can be too?

If you take nothing else from this book, just remember that it's OK to be a bit shit sometimes. Normalising failure, not catastrophising it, is a major gift to yourself and all those around you. It also helps you recover from failure quicker and learn from it faster so it kind of leads to more successful places in the end. Nobody sets out to fail, but we could be a whole lot better at dealing with it when it happens.

Also, allowing our places and our projects to be a little bit crap, makes them so much more of an inviting and human place to be. Don't strive for perfection unless you want somebody shouting in a kitchen somewhere!

Is your environment a human one?

Is it time to break out the fairy lights?! Ask yourself what you are saying to people who come into your space, before anyone has opened their mouth.

Decor says a lot. We talked, for instance, about how all the places we go in times of crisis are scary. How do we convey trust with a chair? How does our carpet say we value you ... or not?!

Will you sit down with more people you disagree with?

Maybe this is the question on which the future of our world depends the most! I didn't offer you any clever strategies here, beyond just not putting the expectation of reaching consensus or agreement. It's OK to just sit in disagreement, but still be alongside each other. Two differing opinions can occupy the same space. If it's too awkward then talk about something else, something less contentious. If we see each other as human, it's a start to reducing that social distance that my friend and hero Srdja Popovic said was the answer.

That's a lot to remember. OK then I'll make it easy for you. In Camerados we've just slashed it down to six things to use. They are the Camerados principles. See the pic at the end of this chapter.

I keep waiting for them to be debunked, but they've been used by many communities far and wide and people still tell us they love them. They are not rules, they are just things to try.

No doubt like me you'll be pretty shit at them most days, but hey, that's on message! They are not *instead of* what you do already, I hope they compliment and turbo boost your brilliant self. They can just sit *alongside* your life and be useful when you need them.

If you want to talk about them, challenge them, add to them or bring them to life artistically (yes please!) do get in touch ... again my email is maff@Camerados.org.

Please also remember that you don't have to do stuff on your own. Connection means sharing the load with a group – we never suggest people set up a public living room on their own. Grab a pal or two, make it fun and the week you can't make it ask somebody else to help, they'll probably love that. If you make it fun and light you'll want to do it again.

It doesn't have to be a public living room. You may not want to do that. That might not be your jam. So do something else. Find other approaches, other ideas. There's loads out there. Follow us on social media, we shout about other movements we love. I have struggled to write this book for six years. It has had many iterations and many times it has been thrown in the bottom drawer. One of the main difficulties was coming to terms with the fact I was going to be doing all the talking. I have become more and more self-conscious about the inevitably narcissistic exercise of writing a book of your ideas. It's like shouting at someone for hours, so if it has ever felt like that I want to say I'm very sorry, it wasn't my intention. I also am very aware that the last thing the world needs is another white, privileged man saying what he thinks. I have, however, finally written this because many women, many people of colour have told me to use my platform to get these ideas out there. So thanks to them for nudging me. I still find it uncomfortable but I have them in my mind as I write this and you'll find some of their names in the acknowledgements. So when you put this book down I wish you the very best in finding your own friends and purpose if you haven't got it already. If you do, treasure it a little more maybe.

But remember.

Whatever you do,

make sure you are just a little bit shit! Keep it human.

Your camerado, Maff

THE 6 CAMERADOS IDEAS (WE ALSO CALL THESE OUR PRINCIPLES)

MIX WITH PEOPLE WHO ARE NOT LIKE YOU

IT'S OK TO DISAGREE RESPECTFULLY

NO FIXING - JUST BE ALONGSIDE ONE ANOTHER

ASK SOMEONE WHO IS STRUGGLING TO HELP YOU

IT'S OK TO BE A BIT RUBBISH SOMETIMES

#WEARECAMERADOS

TO BE SILLY IS TO BE HUMAN

CAMERADOS.ORG

MY VERY LONG AND INDULGENT ACKNOWLEDGEMENTS

Please skip this if indulgent gratitude bores you! You probably won't know who these people are but they will.

First and foremost I must thank the people who sat down. I've changed most of the names of the folks I spoke to on the streets and in a small number of cases changed their location too, but all the details were absolutely true as I heard them. I send my most massive thanks to all of those people who shared my sofa out there. Without them half this book wouldn't exist, obviously. Also none of them reported me to the police so, you know, that was nice of them.

Roc Sandford and Alex Lockwood who broke my book deadlock and did everything to help me get this out—I cannot thank you enough. Without the knowledge and encouragement of these two guys you wouldn't be holding this book. Roc's grandfather published books too and used a font especially designed by famous artist Eric Gill (he of Gill Sans!!) called *Golden Cockerel*. In honour of Roc and his Grandad you are reading that font now and throughout this book.

Thank you Victoria Herriman whose astonishing illustrations light up this book. She is so crazily talented that we had to employ her. I urge you to work with her too – victoria@Camerados.org. Thanks for being my book camerado, Victoria. I would say "we took this journey together" but then I'd have to shoot myself in the face for being an enormous wanker for using that corny metaphor.

Fran East for proof reading with precision and thoughtfulness (hire her folks - I can put you in touch!); Professor Beth Williamson B.A.(Oxon.) M.A., Ph.D. (Lond.) who wrote alongside me (on zoom) in the early days with her trademark unflappable patience for neurotic men; Dr Martha Newson, BSc, MSc, AFHEA, DPhil who helped me so much by thinking stuff through and would have lent this book much needed scholarly gravitas had she written it with me (next time mate, when you're less in demand!); Liam Black, author and friend, whose brave voice gave me the mettle to speak my own mind in these pages and even though he gives me huge amounts of shit, constantly, unabating, relentless (Jesus!!) I know it is really loyal friendship and encouragement (it is isn't it Liam?!!!); Matt Nixon, author, friend and hepcat, who read the book in one sitting and looked beyond the obvious deficiencies of a rough draft, a real skill, to give me insights and lovely words that gave me the last bit of juice to finally get this done. And of course Srdja Popovic. We've only met once and spoken a bunch of times so perhaps he thinks I'm some kind of Travis Bickle character fixated on him!! I'm not, honestly, but this is how inspiration works, someone's words and ideas can seem small but explode inside you with massive effect and give you strangely powerful permission and ripple outwards to affect others too, exponentially for years and years ... and that's what this odd Serb did for me. Thanks Srdja.

Thank you to the first person and the last who helped me get this done. Firstly Tony McKenzie, great friend from school days and proprietor of the World's Most Beautiful Bed & Breakfast (www.woodhousebuttermere. uk) in the Lakes, where I started writing this book. His cooking and good craic each evening were the sustenance my doubting mind required. And the last people who made the final excruciating decisions easier, my brilliant pals Paul Whitty & Hazel Waeland who finally laid the doubting mind to rest.

Jenny Fox was my most ardent encourager and believer back when I started the book six years ago(!!). She also happens to be the person whose door I knocked on when I couldn't get anywhere launching the movement in that first year. Flogging up and down the country in cars strewn with (illicit) KFC wrappers convincing folk to give this thing a punt without having a clue what it was ourselves ... and rabbiting on and on and on together about what this movement could be ... it was just about the best time ever. Except when we realised we'd talked so much that we'd ended up in St Albans. No Jenny = no Camerados, simple as that.

Thanks to the team at the Association of Camerados who put up with me complaining about not getting the book done - alright already!! The Beaver (Yvonne Dawson) for being the best water dwelling mammal I've ever worked with, more capable and kind than an otter for sure, a legend; Elizabeth the self-confessed (brilliant) bean counter; Vikki who sends all the boxes around the world and packs them so lovingly by hand; Helen Parker who left the corporate world to join us and was last seen wearing a pantomime horse costume to lead a workshop ... I think we got to her! Wonderful woman and brilliant adviser. And in fact all the folk who moulded this movement in our first ten years, bonkers and passionately driven folk: Sarah BC, Emma, Izzy, Tim M, Rachel, Lissa, Mabel, Chris, Catherine "The Shoopery" Wilkes (check out The Shoopery.com), Maria, the ever present, do anything, go anywhere Steve "legend" Foster, our landlady without whom we'd be homeless Elizabeth Gordon of Well House(!) and all the wonderfully kind staff in our early experimental cafés and Neighbourhood Kitchens. I must thank the early directors of our not-for-profit Community Interest Company who did the early big thinking and tea drinking: Elle, Stephen and the great Nerys Parry. Wonderfully generous pals Elle & Stephen also designed the logo and brand for our movement (in the pub as previously mentioned) and the impact of that work is immeasurable, it means so much to so many people now.

Thank you to the current directors too. Two of the most fearless people you could ever have on your side and who were asked to be directors because their level of integrity is only matched by their talent at challenging and questioning (and supporting) me! Thank you Bob Thust and Kal Kay.

Did I get this far down the *Acknowledgements* without thanking our funders?! Our team is deliberately tiny and cheap so we can put mission before preservation. We also need to keep our ability to be nimble and constantly iterate according to the needs of the movement. However, that requires funders with advanced levels of insight, intelligence and risk appetite. If I wore hats I would take them all off many times to Dav and the folks at National Community Lottery Fund; Nicky Lappin at Tudor Trust; the Esmée Fairbairn gang and most of all to the ones who stood by us first and remained there throughout, the small but mighty Lankelly Chase Foundation. Julian sat in a park with me and said he would back me, that day changed everything, it allowed me to give this a go and not lose my house. Lankelly's Jess and Joe were the regular human face and became the best partners we could have had. Most funders are "fund and forget" funders, not these guys, they wanted to keep in touch and so did we.

We've also had a raft of genius associates, suppliers, partners and lovely work-experience kids from the local school too! It takes a lot of folk pouring a lot of their heart and soul in to get a global movement creaking into existence and fumbling along eh?!

All thanks ultimately though lead back to my wife Ruth. Fierce critic and yet my soulmate. Nobody convinced me more that connection can turn a life around. She did that for me a country mile more than any other person in my life. Also to my sons Fred, Herbie and Sonny. They've all come out on the streets with me and all too often they have lugged furniture from the lock up for their arthritic husband and Dad. I halved our household income and spent many hours away from them to get this dream going and so obviously it belongs to Ruth and the boys too.

As it also belongs TO EVERYONE who gives it a go in their neighbourhood from Wisconsin to Wiltshire and other places that don't begin with W. All of you reading this and maybe talking to others about the ideas are contributing, and I hope you're making it your own. Although it's yours and ours I'm still grateful to you for being interested. Honestly my wife doesn't even trust me to drive her to the shops so giving this whole Camerados thing your time is very good of you, cheers!

Maff xxx

GET INVOLVED
CAMERADOS.ORG
#WEARECAMERADOS